Penguin Book
GREG MATTHEW

While studying Law and Arts at the Univer
Roland Fishman played first grade Rugby
athletics, sailed in the Sydney-Hobart and surfed. Despite this he
graduated and after travelling overseas, returned to work on the
Financial Review. He became a sports writer on the *Sydney Morning
Herald* and has most recently been writing features for *Good
Weekend*.

GREG MATTHEWS

The Spirit of Modern Cricket

Roland Fishman

PENGUIN BOOKS

Penguin Books Australia Ltd,
487 Maroondah Highway, P.O. Box 257
Ringwood, Victoria, 3134, Australia
Penguin Books Ltd,
Harmondsworth, Middlesex, England
Penguin Books,
40 West 23rd Street, New York, N.Y. 10010, U.S.A.
Penguin Books Canada Limited,
2801 John Street, Markham, Ontario, Canada L3R 1B4
Penguin Books (N.Z.) Ltd,
182-190 Wairau Road, Auckland 10, New Zealand

First published by Penguin Books Australia, 1986

Typeset in 90% Garamond by Leader Composition Pty Ltd
Made and printed in Australia by The Dominion Press-Hedges & Bell

Fishman, Roland, 1955- .
Greg Matthews: the spirit of modern cricket.

ISBN 0 14 010020 2.

I. Matthews, Greg, 1959- . 2. Cricket players –
Australia – Biography. I. Title.

796.35'8'0924

CONTENTS

ON THE EDGE

It was 11 November 1985, Remembrance Day, when Australia resumed its second innings in the First Test against New Zealand at the Gabba in Brisbane. When the bugler played the last post at 11 am, it could well have been for Australian cricket.

At one stage Australia were three for 16. Then five for 67. Richard Hadlee, the great all-rounder, appeared unstoppable. Australia had no answers. Andrew Hilditch, the South Australian opener who could not stop himself hooking, hooked and was out for 12. He hung his head in shame as he walked off. He would not bat for Australia again that summer.

Things got worse. Greg Ritchie never looked comfortable. He fenced in no man's land off a delivery from Martin Snedden and was easily caught at second slip. Wayne Phillips chopped a Hadlee delivery into his stumps and was out for two. Allan Border, the captain of the team, seemed to be the only Australian capable of putting up any sort of fight. He was 26 not out when Australia had lost five wickets. He needed someone to stay with him.

Enter Greg Matthews. New Zealand had made five for 553 in their first innings. Australia had managed 179. There were nearly two days to play. Greg was the only recognised batsman to come in.

Matthew's personal predicament was as grim. Before the Test a headline in the Sydney *Sun* read, GREG MUST GO. Matthews said, 'I was on the edge so to speak. I knew they were looking for people to drop. I knew it could well be me.'

His mother, Neita, said the hardest thing about Test cricket was that the players were so scared of getting dropped that some were physically ill before they went out. If they only had a bit more security when they started, the death rate among young Test players might not be so high.

Matthews thought his chances of being picked for the First Test against New Zealand were so slim that he told his brother, Peter, that it would be alright for Peter's first child to be christened on the day the match started. He was probably the tenth or eleventh player picked.

In the first innings Matthews had been surprised he did not feel nervous. He felt quite comfortable at the crease and was pleased when he scored two to get off the mark. His cool disposition was of little assistance. Hadlee bowled him for two. But Matthews was not too uptight about this as his dismissal was the result of fine bowling not dismal batting.

The ball that got him was a beauty. It pitched just outside the off stump at an almost perfect length and seamed back towards the wicket. Matthews did everything right but the ball bounced over his knee and clipped the top of the stumps. He remembered what his mentor Gordon Nolan had said, 'If it just clips the top of the stumps, it is a good delivery.'

It still hurt. Failure at cricket wounds Matthews more than most. Cricket is his passion and profession. He had been a full-time professional for five years and had no other career prospects. When he walked out for the second innings, he knew he was on the edge.

Bill O'Reilly in action

YESTERDAY'S HEROES

The meeting of the old and the new can be interesting. When Bill O'Reilly, who played cricket for Australia half-a-century ago, met Greg in Melbourne, it was a meeting of two worlds. O'Reilly was in town to write his column on the cricket Tests between Pakistan and Australia for the *Sydney Morning Herald* and the Melbourne *Age*. When he ran into Greg, dressed in his civilian clothes, O'Reilly thought, 'Christ what is this?'

In O'Reilly's day, those who represented their country dressed as businessmen, wore suits and ties, had the same regulation haircuts and never wore earrings. O'Reilly was having his breakfast at the Hilton, which he says is not a bad pub, when this strange looking bloke came up to him wearing loud sunglasses, a coat which hung below his knees and had what O'Reilly described as long and scraggly hair. 'He looked like something the cat dragged in.'

That was off the field. On the field Greg was the talk of the country after scoring 75 in his Test debut before protesting loudly when given out leg-before-wicket at the Melbourne Cricket Ground. Everyone associated with the game, including Greg, agreed the outburst was not quite cricket.

With all the publicity the incident generated, Greg could reasonably expect to be recognised by anyone who followed the game. So when he spotted O'Reilly he thought he would take the opportunity to renew his brief acquaintance with the ex-great. He did not think it would be necessary to re-introduce himself. He stuck out his paw.

'Who are you?' O'Reilly said.

'Greg Matthews' came the reply.

O'Reilly was taken aback. But he had been through the bodyline series and thrown into new situations before. It was not cricket to make a fuss about how a bloke was dressed in a pub.

'Well done,' O'Reilly said, referring to Greg's cricket.

They had a quick chat. Greg went about his business. O'Reilly finished his breakfast and continued talking about the lack of good spin bowlers.

Greg, who is more likely to do something than think about it, was less affected by the encounter than O'Reilly. 'Once, after a match Mr O'Reilly had said to come and have a chat with him if I saw him about,' Greg said, 'so I did. I enjoyed talking to him. He is from a different time. Has different thoughts. He has seen a lot of cricket.'

While not seeing Greg as a potential soul-mate, O'Reilly is enthusiastic about Greg the cricketer. The first time he saw Greg play was in a Sheffield Shield match at the Sydney Cricket Ground against Western Australia. He thought Greg had the best two qualities any young man could have – concentration and enthusiasm. 'I didn't think he had any more natural ability than the run-of-the-mill good Shield player . . . The only thing I want to know about you is whether you have concentration and enthusiasm. If you have those two qualities you can't be stopped. You are hard to beat at anything. Cricket is a bit like making love to a girl. If you are not determined you will not get to first base. The Duke of Wellington had nothing more going for him other than concentration and enthusiasm. Look where it got him. Matthews has got no more ability as a batsman than I had and I used to go in at number eleven.'

O'Reilly does not really mind what a young cricketer does when he walks off the paddock, but nevertheless Matthews, the human being, has created quite an impression on O'Reilly. 'He is a bit of a weirdo. Not the sort of person most Australians can relate to. I have never met, or should I say noticed, anyone like him. He is a real one-offer. Most people like their heroes to conform. I don't know that I would like to spend a day with him.'

O'Reilly reflects the ambivalence of sections of the establishment. Nevertheless, in many ways Greg's extraordinary popularity had to happen. Cricket is now marketed to appeal to the young and is riddled with such innovations as colourful outfits, white balls, bright lights at night venues, instant one-day excitement and pop music promotions, unimagineable even in the early seventies. It would be ridiculously optimistic to expect the player heroes to remain the same.

The game is slipping from the establishment. At best they share it with the kids for whom the heavy one-day cricket schedule was introduced. Cricket connoisseurs, including most of the current players, prefer Tests to one-dayers.

Lynton Taylor, the managing director of PBL Marketing which promotes international cricket in Australia, said the players preferred Tests because there were plenty of breaks in play and they were less physically demanding than the one-dayers. Regardless of their preference, they have to play one-dayers whether they like it or not. They pay the wages bill.

Bob Simpson, who commentates for the ABC, finds the one-dayers boring because for him they are so predictable. They are very difficult to call as the field settings are often the same, the action repetitive and, as they often depend on the result for their excitement, you could go to sleep, wake up half-an-hour from the end and take up the commentary. Even though the one-dayers are supposed to provide excitement throughout, the results are often a foregone conclusion after 15 overs. Defensive cricket often wins the day.

This may be, but Tests can be as boring as watching an America's Cup yacht race without having a boat to cheer for. 'A really absorbing battle going on here . . . He just pushes it wide of mid-off . . . a better delivery . . . again there is no run . . . Lillee bowling to Greig . . . Two, slips, a gully, mid-off, cover, extra cover . . . He pushes that wide of mid-off. The batsmen go through for a single. That takes Greig on to 7, England to 356 and Lillee's figures now three wicket for 110.

'Yes Ritchie it is a glorious day . . . I would just like to take this opportunity to say hello . . . '

In contrast the moment by moment involvement in one day matches is similar to that of American sports where every play seems important. In one-day games there is a run rate which gives the activity on the field a more defined purpose. The drama builds, the commentators have something relevant to talk about and a result is assured.

But is it cricket as the civilised world knows it? The former

Australian captain who became leader of the rebel tour to South Africa in 1985, Kim Hughes, believes the game and its administration has changed too much for its own good. 'I think the game at home is a shambles', he said when he was in South Africa. 'I think with the resources we have got we should be the best cricketing country in the world. At the moment we're what, fifth or sixth? ... Its the marketing people that run it – it's PBL. I don't criticise them. They did a business deal with the Board which was fantastic, unbelieveable ... The important decisions in cricket are made for marketing reasons. But who watches our game any more?'

Good question. As the game has changed the people who watch have changed and the heroes change. In the days of Bill O'Reilly the game belonged to the most conservative of the establishment. Then along came Ian Chappell and his lads. They took cricket from the yachting set and gave it to the blokes in jeans. The game was then dominated by brash moustacheoed ockers. They were arrogant, competitive and fine cricketers who were increasingly interested in making money. Their decision to play for Kerry Packer's World Series Cricket changed the game – its audience, its administration – forever and made sure established Test cricketers would be quite well off.

The world and cricket have changed again. Rock and Roll is the music of the era. In the last American presidential election commentators began talking about the Springsteen factor. In advertising, the energy and broad appeal of rock music is used to sell anything and everything. Rock no longer lives on the fringe of most people's world, even if some of those that have run the game think that it is a threat to the moral fibre of the nation. Such people don't remotely relate to rock heroes. They prefer young men fashioned in their own old-fashioned image.

But a look at other sports gives an idea of the influence of the rock image. The most blatant is Rock and Roll Wrestling, but the less absurd sports have also been infiltrated. During the 1986 Wimbledon, Channel 9 led into its commercial breaks with tennis images and a rock refrains. 'Wide World of Sports' and telecasts of Grand Prix motor racing do the same. Pat Cash currently Australia's most

The Australian team after a match against Pakistan, 1973

successful and popular tennis player with his passion for Twisted Sister ('We Can't be Beaten'), head bands and adoring groupies, has the image of a heavy-metal base guitarist.

Greg has given cricket to the rock generation who are quite happy to appear to be different and be seen at the cricket. They now have someone to whom they can directly relate. The saying that a good suit will never be out of fashion no longer holds in many circles. Channel 9 has given Greg his own video which features Greg batting, bowling, leaping in the air, pulling faces, dancing and hugging teammates to the sound of the Hoodoo Gurus song 'Like Wow Wipeout'. The papers have called Greg a disco kid and a punk rocker, quite a contradiction in terms.

Before Greg emerged, cricket stars were not really made of the stuff to turn on the hip young souls of the eighties. Test cricketers tended to have personalities in the lawyer and accountant mode. The biggest stars in the first half of the eighties were Dennis Lillee, Rod Marsh, Allan Border and Greg Chappell. Their image was a bit straight for the new youngsters who had been turned onto cricket. Lillee, with his gold chain and John Newcombe moustache, looks like an advertising executive, Border has the dour demeanour and clipped moustache of a junior army officer and Greg Chappell's on-and-off field aloofness gave him the image of a high-ranking insurance executive.

In contrast, Greg Matthews looks and acts like a big kid. 'He's like us,' an unnamed 17-year-old told Sue Mott of the *Australian*. 'He's just unreal,' another worshipper said. There is no doubting Greg's high ranking in the cult stakes. He gets a standing ovation for doing nothing more than walking onto the field. In a one-day match at the Gabba against India the crowd wildly chanted his name as if they were cajoling a rock star onto the stage for an encore. Bill O'Reilly describes the ovation Greg receives as Bradmanesque.

The newspapers have played up Greg's elevated status. A headline in the *Australian* read, 'Matthews the cure for cricket's depression.' Richard Cashman, a cricket historian, wrote in the *National Times* in January 1986, 'He is now firmly established as cricket's latest folk hero.

Ian Chappell and Doug Walters at Sydney Airport bound for the West
Indies, 1972

Some have gone a little over the top. 'Epitomising the spirit of each age', Cashman wrote, 'helps the hero to both capture the public imagination and to regenerate faith in the Australian team, the game itself and society and the nation too.' Thank God for Greg.

'Exuberant and energetic', Cashman continues, 'Matthews, seemingly inspired by the punk, disco and aerobic movement, reflecting the cult of fitness, the new determination to work hard and a more professional approach to sport seems to mirror the rhythms and moods of the hungry eighties. He also seems willing to accept the mantle of cult figure and the mission to lift the flagging spirits of the country's long-suffering cricket fans.'

Greg is not so sure of the reason for his popularity. 'Can you tell me why people find me so interesting all of a sudden?' he asked me the first time I met him. 'All sorts of people come up to me and say they have wanted to meet me for a long time. I am buggered if I know why.'

Modern journalists seek in-depth features and are pressured to beat-up what they get to sharpen their stories. This makes it harder for anyone, whether politician or sportsman, to achieve the status of former heroes. Between 1930 and 1960 sportswriters such as Neville Cardus and Oscar Robertson made sportsmen heroic figures. The warts and any other unsavoury traits were covered with a thick layer of makeup. Victor Trumper, a Test cricketer at the turn of the century, was portrayed as a modest man whose humility bordered on saintliness. He was so eulogised that it was only recently that biographers have been able to find a human side to him. If Ian Botham were a star player 40 years ago, he would probably have the dashing young man-about-town image of a Keith Miller.

Greg is unimpressed with the writers of today. He feels they either lack deep knowledge of the game, over-write or are too quick to criticise. But he recognises that they, like the radio and television commentators, have a hard job to do – churning out information day-in day-out about the never ending cricket season. He quite likes to listen to the commentaries of matches on the radio, but his teammates want it off.

It is far more than the writers who have changed. Today international cricket dominates the sports world in Australia from the beginning of summer to the end. The games and plays seem to roll into one another. Longtime cricket followers say they find it easier to remember events that happened in the early fifties than something which happened in the never ending summer of '85.

If the combat is spread out the great deeds tend to stand out more. In the days of the pre-global village, England played here once every four years and Australia went to Great Britain every four years. A Test Match was a real event. Fine deeds on the field seemed ridiculously important and lived on and on.

But it was not just through cricket that Greg became a cult hero. He is a fine Test cricketer, but his popularity came before his real success on the field. If a best-ever Australian team were selected from all those who played to the end of 1986, Greg would not get a look-in. It is almost certain he would not be named in a World Eleven for that year. By his own admission, in early 1986 he was not yet ready for the power of the West Indies.

Cashman analyses yesterday's folk heroes to help us understand why Greg has been able to join the elite band of Frederick Spofforth, Victor Trumper, Keith Miller and Dougie Walters. Lillee and Ian Chappell miss out. They were great cricketers and household names but they never had that something that captures the imagination of a generation.

Walters is the most recently retired cult hero. His casualness and style gave him universal appeal. He was the bloke who loved a beer, a smoke, or a game of poker as much as anything. He was the sporting Paul Hogan. Stories sprung up about Walters.

> "Did you hear about the time when Dougie got the call to bat in the middle of a card game?
> No.
> Well, he has a good hand when the call to bat comes, so he makes his bet, rests his still burning cigarette on the ash tray, smiles and says: 'Hang on fellas I'll be back in a minute.' And you know what? He was back to play out the hand.
> No.

19

Doug Walters, national serviceman, 1966

Well, did you hear about the time Dougie's wife rang the dressing room just after he had gone in to bat?

No.

Well, one of the players answered the phone and told her: 'Dougie has just gone in,' and she said, 'I'll wait.'

No. But I'll tell you what that 100 he scored against New Zealand was one of the best innings I have ever seen."

The secret of humour and folkherohood is, pause, timing. Walters' career coincided with Hogan and the ocker cult. Spofforth made his name when Australia first entered the Test arena. His 14 wickets and 90 runs at Lords in 1882 made sure that his name would not be lost in the ashes. Trumper was a working class hero who first played Test cricket just prior to Federation when Australians were looking for heroes. Bradman's most brilliant season was in 1930 when people sought diversions to escape the gloom of the depression. That year he helped reverse the English dominance in the 1928-29 series. Bradman was then at the Australian centre of the bodyline series, the first to be broadcast play-by-play on radio. The first hero of the post-Bradman era was Keith Miller whose nonchalant attitude and notorious off-field lifestyle excited the worshippers of the day. Bill O'Reilly, the great leg spin bowler of the Bradman era, said of Miller, 'He was a real man of the world. He was the sort of man who could always pull something out of the bag to suit the occasion. If the batsmen needed a ball around the ear 'ole, Miller would give it to them.'

Walters was the last of the line and no-one had stepped in to take his place. Australian cricket was going nowhere. Ockerism had become a successful marketing device in the United States to lure tourists, but it was not the image the young cricket followers aspired to anymore.

After the success of the Australian America's Cup campaign, the sporting public seems to want more from its athletes. Heroic failure was now seen as no success at all. People wanted someone who would hustle for perfection. The she'll – be – right attitude was not enough.

Keith Miller at the SCG, 1972

Cashman agrees that something different was required for the eighties. 'Ockerism was far less relevant in the meaner tougher eighties. Everyone realised that runs, and for that matter jobs, could not be had by shaking the proverbial pagoda tree. Australian fans yearned for another cricketing incarnation ... Cricket heroes like the ten incarnations of the Hindu God Vishnu, seem to materialise miraculously when they are most needed.'

A BUNDLE OF CONTRADICTIONS

People don't know quite what to make of Greg Matthews. In one sense he is yesterday's hero – the young man who has dedicated his life to cricket. While still on the fringe of the big money he was offered tax-free $200,000 to play in South Africa but chose to remain in Australia – not to help undermine apartheid, but to enable him to represent his country at Lords, in Pakistan, against the West Indies, anywhere.

Yet Greg is the hip young man of the eighties. His dress, language and personality are so different from the traditional cricketer, or regular guy in the street for that matter, that he is bound to stand out anywhere. But he is more than just a whacky eccentric. He is a classic cricketer who has devoted much of his life to his craft. His attitude is an inspiration to his teammates, cricket followers and anyone else who wants to achieve.

He never lets up. If it is 120 degrees in the water-bag at Adelaide Oval and the opposition are three for 380 on the last day when a draw seems inevitable, most players relax and let the game run its inevitable course. Not Greg. He will run down the ball to save the extra run, race into position at the change of overs, clap his hands and say, 'Come on. Hustle. Remember your responsibilities. If we take a wicket now they will crumble. Come on what's wrong with you guys . . . I don't mean to tell you your job or anything, but don't you think you should be bowling at off stump . . . Think about it.'

His enthusiasm is infectious. The NSW team for whom he plays have dominated the Sheffield Shield competition. In the 1985-86 season the Australian team under Allan Border began to pull together and show some fight. Team morale rose significantly. Greg was a big part of the new spirit. Other players began looking to him for advice, inspiration and performances.

Greg is the classic cricket enthusiast, but not from the classic mould. Music really turns him on. After Jillian his 'favourite relaxation' is listening and bopping to rock music. 'The Oils are great, Talking Heads are my band of the moment, Jillian turned me on to them. I like Sade, Style Council, Sting, who I did not have a big wrap on before I met Jillian. She studied music and really knows her stuff. I find it hard to argue with her on the subject. Joe Cocker, I like. Deep Purple ... best gig I have ever been to ... black and white sound ... unbelievable ... so tight and strong ... Dire Straights ... I have seen them live three times ... I saw them in a small gig at Wembley, very disappointing light show. They are too funky and drony. Jillian understands what I mean by drony. I hope you do.'

After a heavy night he enjoys classical music. 'It is great on the ear and braincells.' Before a game he pumps himself up with rock music, the Oils in particular give him the power and the passion to succeed. It is ironic that Greg's favourite Australian band is one of the country's most political yet Greg is quite unwilling to express any political views publicly. You almost get the feeling that the worst thing about a nuclear war, for Greg, would be that a Test series against the West Indies could be cancelled, just when he was running hot.

Music is a useful tool for Greg's cricket. He has played back-up bat to David Bowie. Bowie was running through a few songs rehearsing at the Sydney Sports Ground when New South Wales were playing Pakistan next door at the Sydney Cricket Ground. Greg got a charge from the music and was dancing and strumming his bat in time to the music on his way to an impressive 86.

He says the dancing and singing are not for show. It is for him. He does it because it is good for his game. The music and other antics help him relax. It takes his mind off the game temporarily and, after a quick mental tea-break, he comes back to the action with a fresher mind and sharper edge.

The lucky souls who field in the slips get their mind temporarily off the game by talking and sharing the odd bad joke with a nearby teammate. Poor old Greg is usually out in the covers all alone and has to amuse himself. He often relieves the tedium by chatting to someone in the crowd. During one game Greg spotted an old mate of his, Ken Gentles, about 30 metres away in the stands at the SCG. Greg had read in the papers that Gentles had done well for Greg's old club Parramatta in a match the previous weekend. There was a break in play.

Greg waved and yelled out: 'Well bowled on Saturday. WELL DONE.'

Someone in the crowd screamed: 'You lair Matthews.'

Greg smiled and gave an elegant bow.

All good fun and good for Greg's cricket. But there has been so much fuss made of his on-field antics that he feels self-conscious about them. He has toned down that part of his act considerably. Partly because he wants to be talked about and remembered as a cricketer not as a whacky guy who happens to play cricket. And partly because he says other people deserve publicity too. Besides, clown princes do not have the stuff from which Australian captains are perceived to be made of. Rod Marsh was always seen as a bit of a larrikin by the selectors and never led his country when many thought he was the best man for the job.

But whether he likes to admit it or not, one thing Greg is, is a good showman. He will use anything for a stage and anyone for an audience. He loved playing fullback in Rugby Union because it gave him the chance to be out there alone and make great covering tackles. 'Everything you do at fullback is accentuated'. Greg will be himself and play the part of Greg Matthews whether he is talking to an anonymous telephone operator from a cab company or chatting to the Prime Minister's wife at Kirribilli House. What you see on the tele is what you get in the flesh – a crazy, zany, hyperactive guy, who would have trouble sitting still in a dentist's chair. If he were faking it, the Greg Matthews' show would not work well on television.

When Greg was the focus of a '60 Minutes' segment pronouncing him a folk hero, he was a natural. We saw clips of him hugging teammates, clowning in the dressing room, cooking up a storm at home, canoodling with Jillian, pulling faces on the field and chatting with Hazel Hawke, whom Greg found himself next to at a function for the Australian Cricket team. It can be tough to know where to begin with a famous stranger at a public function. Such encounters are often stilted and awkward. Not so with Greg. He brushed his hand through his hair and said: 'Do you get to spend much time in Sydney?' Not overly original, but the conversation developed from there.

By the end of the '60 Minutes' interview Greg was in full stride when a straight-faced George Negus asked the last question of the segment – 'What is the Greg Matthews' personality really like?' A tough one. Sum yourself up in 15 seconds. If you take yourself too seriously you are a dag, but nothing is worse than forced humour. There is no time to think. Luckily spontaneity is Greg's forte. After a millisecond's thought Greg gave his head a wiggle, pulled a goofy face, and said: 'I'm a great guy.' Greg giggles. The segment cuts to a ticking clock.

Greg was out of town playing cricket when the show went to air, so he missed seeing it. He phoned Jillian.

'Hello, Clarkie, how did '60 Minutes' go?'

'OK,' she said.

'Did we get any laughs?' Greg asks.

'A few,' Jillian said. 'A lot of people said they liked it.'

Greg was pleased, but for him the most important show in town is cricket. Cricket and Jillian, depending on the time of day and season, are the passions and focus of Greg's life. He has wanted to play Test cricket for as long as he can remember. He has never really wanted to be anything other than a cricketer. Vocational guidance questionnaires at school failed to reveal any standard career path for him. Greg's brother Peter said if Greg was not a successful cricketer he could be struggling.

Greg found his Jillian at the NSW Cricketers Club and has not really wanted to spend his spare time with anyone else since. More often than not the two spend their nights in front of the television, listening to music or talking.

28

Greg is so passionate about cricket he is like a character from *Tom Brown's Schooldays*.

'I love running out there, I don't care if it is 200 degrees. It's the best place in the world to be. Some of the guys say on hot days, "I wish I was at the beach." I would not be there for quids. No way. I would not swap this for anything. It is my own world sort of. It's a rare occurrence playing Test Cricket. It does not last forever and it does not happen to everyone. It is an important time . . . Cricket is more than a game to me.'

Playing Test cricket has been such a long standing Greg Matthews' dream that the realisation of the dream is a little hard to wake up to at times.

'I have played Test cricket for Australia. It just blows me away. I never thought I would do it. I always thought I would play first class cricket. But I did not think I would play Test cricket until my first first class game. Then I knew. I knew I would play for Australia no problem. Well, I knew there would be a problem, but I knew I was good enough. When I was young and watched Australia play on television I thought every bowler bowled every ball like Dennis Lillee and every batsman batted like Greg Chappell.'

Reality did not prove as daunting as the dream.

'But when you get out there with them you realise they are just eleven dudes out there representing their country. I looked at the personnel and I knew I was good enough. They are all human and not as good as I had built them up to be.'

With Jillian it was love at first sight. Bells were ringing when they first met. Greg would tell her: 'The hills are alive . . . The hills are alive.' Today they are still ringing. 'She is the best woman I have ever known', he said. 'She is the best at everything, she is just the best?' But more of Jillian later.

Greg does not just want to be in the Australian side to make up the numbers. He desperately wants to do his bit for his country. To him, while winning is everything, it is not the only thing. He would be horribly frustrated if the opening batsmen scored all the runs and the opening bowlers took all the wickets. He loves the process and the fight. His mum says if Greg had been born in the days of King Arthur he would have been a knight ready to lay down his life for his king and country.

The king and country stuff suggests a misty eyed boy whose values and aspirations don't reflect the eighties. Not so. Greg is aware of the financial benefits which he can derive from cricket and is obsessed with achieving personal goals. Yet he is a great team player. Personal victory is hollow without team success.

This all sounds so noble. But he is not naive. After doing well for Australia one day he was asked whether he had thought of himself or his country foremost during his innings. A dodgy question. If he says, 'I did it for my country,' he sounds like a right jerk as everyone knows cricket is a big business and the players are desperate to stay in the Test team. Much money and pride are at stake. Who can honestly claim they believe in blind nationalism anymore? On the other hand you don't want to say, 'I did it for myself' and sound like an egomaniac. Jillian says Greg is both humble and an egomaniac.

Greg's answer was a beauty. 'I was thinking about myself because I was the person batting. I thought if I did well my country would do well. Basically Greg Matthews had a job to do, not Australia.'

Greg speaks with a language all of his own. He sounds more like a black jazz musician from San Francisco in the 60s than a Sydney athlete. No monosyllabic jock grunting away in mundane cliches here. What you hear from many Australian sportspeople are comments like, 'The hammie feels pretty good ... It was tough out there ... The wicket was pretty good ... I would like to thank Channel 10 and NEC for this award.' Mind you sometimes the questions get the answers they deserve.

The language of Greg Matthews is alive. He has invented his own cliches. He describes Vivian Richards as 'the man.' The Australian Test spinner Bob Holland is 'a sweet man'. Howard Northey, a journalist from Australian Associated Press, is 'a cool dude.' He likes 'rapping' to people. Some cricket matches are referred to as 'gigs'. If he likes something, it 'turns him on'. When he thinks something looks good he likes the 'visuals'. He wears an earring because he likes the visuals.

His favourite superlative is 'sensaysh'. A catch is sensaysh, a band

is sensaysh, a surprise almond croissant is sensayah and Tooheys Old beer is sensaysh. When he answers the phone he says: 'What's happening?' When he hangs up he says, 'Later'. Sensaysh.

Cricket old-timer Bill O'Reilly said: 'It is a brand of English that I have never heard and I was a schoolteacher.'

The Indians had not heard it either. When he was interviewed for an Indian sports magazine, *Sportsworld*, the interview had to be transcribed by four people before they could crack the code.

'Matthews is not a very easy person to interview,' the journalist wrote, 'much of his enthusiasm spills over into the conversation. He speaks so fast it is difficult to follow some of his phrases ... As the Australian wicket keeper, Wayne Phillips, said, "A couple of times I wanted to get an interpreter in to try and work out what he is talking about. He's got a language all of his own." '

The first time I interviewed Matthews for this book, I asked him where his vocabulary came from.

'Everywhere, some words I just like the sound of and start using them.'

For example?

'Well, I will tell you one, but you have to switch the tape recorder off ... I am a bit embarrassed about it.'

The pause button goes on. Greg leans forward. I lean forward. Greg then clearly enunciates the word: 'Zucchini'. Zucchini. We laugh. The pause button goes off.

It is not just what you say it is how you say it. Greg's mother instilled into him the importance of presenting himself well. He can remember her saying to him when he was ten: 'Now Gregory. Shoulders back. Chin up, speak legibly and slowly. There is a way to present yourself ... That's it.'

Greg said: 'You have to present yourself in a certain way. People sometimes see me walking past and think, 'Isn't he a cocky bastard.'. But there is a way to present yourself.'

A friend of mine walked through the room at this time. Greg smiled at her, bounced up on his feet, stuck out his hand and said: 'Greg Matthews ... Lucky I didn't swear. I would have blown my image.'

After she left, he said: 'You have to accommodate all styles. You are a certain style. The garbage collector is a certain style. The old Joe is a certain style. The yobbo who comes up to you in a pub and slaps you on the back is a certain style. You have to wear it for a while and then punch something out that will accommodate him. I have a responsibility. It is part of my job . . . I am getting worse at it.'

This may all sound as though Greg is a contrived character. Not so. He is a very emotional person, who reacts spontaneously and loves his cricket. When he does something he is proud of, he is happy and expresses it. He does not need to attend an encounter group to get in touch with his feelings. They are already just below the surface. It does not take much to get them to bubble forth. Greg cries through sad movies.

Greg would not feel out of place among athletes from the United States who are a demonstrative bunch. American footballers love to hurl a football into the ground or do a dance in the end zone after a touchdown. And if a baseball pitcher gets an unfavourable call from an umpire he is likely to throw his cap to the ground, crowd the umpire and scream things – 'No way you turkey'. It rarely induces the umpire to change his decision but the pitcher feels better and the umpire thinks twice next time. If an American teammate does well his fellow athletes do what they can to make the moment more special for him. 'Alright. Good D (for defence). Way to go?'

When Greg takes a wicket, no matter what the score, it is a big moment, particularly if it is a good delivery to a famous batsman in a Test. After all how many people in the world get to do that? Why not enjoy it? Why not celebrate? Why pretend it is no big deal? If Greg is happy on the field he expresses it. After taking a wicket he is liable to do a war-dance on the pitch, run up to a teammate, rest his head on his shoulder and give him a big hug. Or maybe he will stick his hands out, American basketball style, so a teammate can give him 10. Alright Greg, way to go.

It is infectious. It is fun. It feels good. It gives a team momentum. Other cricketers are now jumping about more. Some will go up to Greg after he or they have done something special and stick their hands out waiting for Greg to give them 10. It is fun to play with an

enthusiast. Positive words and actions induce positive deeds. The successful NSW team have embraced the Matthews style. The NSW pace bowler, Michael Whitney, said: 'We miss Greg when he is not playing . . . There are some guys who stick their hands out for the West Indian style hand-shake only when Greg is there, which is a bit weird. I do it all the time.'

Greg's enthusiasm is fuelled by his passion. 'Cricket is more than a game to me. If they took cricket away from me I would really struggle to exist on earth. Cricket is indescribable. How do you describe an orgasm?'

It is a mystery to everyone, including Greg, why it was sport that got his creative juices flowing as a young chap and kept them running over the years. At school Greg never really shone at anything other than sport. 'I am not proud of my effort at school,' he said. 'I did not make the most of it. I don't want you to play it up. I am not a dummy.'

Few people who get to know him think he is. Manipulative, egocentric and arrogant maybe, but not stupid. He is no great philosopher, but he is as street-wise as the sharpest real estate agent. Those who know him best say he could have made a success of any activity he set his mind to. He has excelled at every athletic endeavour he has turned his attention to. Invariably it was sport which grabbed his attention. He has been told by various people if he did not pursue cricket stardom he could have been a world class golfer, soccer player or rugby player. He even excelled at putt putt.

But cricket is his favourite and why not make money for doing what you love best. As the Dire Straits song says, 'It's money for nothing and your chicks for free.' Other areas of endeavour pale in comparison for Greg. If his thing had been accountancy or carpentry no-one would have questioned his motives, but sport is not perceived as a career path by most Australians. While it would be great to get paid for doing something you love, you have to grow up sometime – or so they say.

That attitude is changing as more money is being invested in sport. Through cricket Greg is going to break free of the wage-slave, mortgage-slave world most of us are sentenced to. Apart from his career path, Greg sees his life plan in conventional terms. Brother Peter has accepted awards for Greg and told the audience that his brother is in many ways a conservative guy. This always gets a laugh. But it is true. He wants to get married and have children by the time he is 30 and use his good fortune to buy a nice house in a good area, hopefully with a backyard for the kids.

Where to buy? 'The Eastern Suburbs turn me on. Paddington turns me on . . . Woollahra really turns me on. Balmain is still a chance. It turns me on, but not as much. I would like to be walking distance to the city for the next five to ten years and then maybe move. Balmain is only ten minutes away. But still ten minutes. You can't have everything. It would be easier to have a backyard in Balmain.' He finally settled on Paddington and was planning to renovate.

Marriage? Children? Backyard for the kids? Is this the person who was described as a punk? Sounds more like a young executive.

Greg comes alive when I question the joy of having children. He leans forward in his seat. 'YEAH' he says and gives me a look as if to say I am loonier than is acceptable. 'That's what we are here for.'

To breed?

'Yeah . . . What the hell do you think you are here for?'

Who knows?

'What do you think you are here for. To breathe the air? To have a good time? The bottom line is you are here to breed, to reproduce. SURVIVAL.'

Oh really.

'Of course. Survival. Otherwise, there would be nothing.'

But surely there are plenty of people in the world.

'Look, it is the individual responsibility of every person to breed. That is the bottom line of why you are here. The survival of the human race . . . Of course.'

Greg gets passionate and then his feelings dissipate. He is not one to expect everyone to agree with his view of the world. When he feels he has made his point and realises he is not going to convert anyone he agrees to disagree. 'Different strokes for different folks,' he says.

Greg with god-daughter Jessica, 1985

There is a gap in the conversation. Greg says to himself, 'It's the beginning.'

It is perhaps a rather uncomplicated view of the world. After all having children is a huge responsibility.

'Yes of course. But I adapt like everything else. Recently I was in Townsville with Jillian and we ran into a couple of friends of hers who have a nine-month-old girl and a three-year-old girl. They have been travelling around Australia in a jeep. When they set off the baby was six months and the girl was two-and-a-half years. The baby adapts. You have to be loving, caring and supportive . . . That's the bottom line. It does not matter where your temple is. As big brother said to me once, it is the quality of love you give your kid, not the quantity, though that is important as well.'

During the meaning of life lecture Greg's body speaks as well as his mouth. His sunglasses are still on. His whole body exudes emotion. In contrast to Greg, most Australian athletes are flat one-dimensional characters. They seem to be on the cultural back burner of society. Making it to the top in sport requires tunnel vision. The dilettante who plays the harp, reads poetry and tends the garden does not have the time or channelled intensity to excel at sport which might explain why many athletes are often a touch narrow. The personality players in Australia are usually the ones who can drink the most beer and tell crude jokes with confidence. Greg only has two jokes which he offered to tell me if I turned the tape recorder off. Australian sportsmen tend to mix with their own kind.

Who are Greg's friends? 'I know a few artists, a few crazies, a few straighties, a few businessmen – licorice all-sorts. I don't like dishonest people who slease around and have a bad aura. I don't like some pretentious people. Some I do because they have a right to be that way because they wear it so well.'

Greg is different from most athletes – or people for that matter. There is no readily available box to put him in. He is very much his own person who varies with the mood and situation. He is a one-off character who can't be characterised. He is a caricature of himself. He is very adaptable but does not change much.

His attitude to some forms of training are not jock-like in the conventional sense. I let on that it is fun to run. 'Running. Oh mate I think people who do that are sick. These gigs who get into marathons I think they are sick. Running around destroying their bodies. Different folks for different strokes and all that. But running. Putting one foot in front of the other. I can't relate to that. Head down going through horrible mental and physical stresses. No thank you.'

One aspect of his personality that has endeared him to the sporting public, his enthusiasm, stands out so much because we live in a society and a time where people like to give the impression they can succeed without trying. In sport the stoic is king. Greg does not mind being the one-out enthusiast. He will be trying just as hard on the field at 6 pm as he was when play started at 11 am.

Peter Roebuck, opening batsman and captain of the English county side Somerset and a fine cricket writer, is so taken by the Matthews approach that he used an old Winston Churchill analogy to sum up Greg's attitude.

At a school speechday Churchill was the guest speaker. The audience expected something profound, pithy and witty. He got up, stared at the crowd and said, 'Never give up. Never give up. Never give up.'

Roebuck said, 'Matthews brings a little of this spirit to every team in which he plays.'

In a Test against India, Greg beat Shastri with a floater. The ball was edged between David Hookes in the slips and the Australian wicket keeper, Wayne Phillips. Hookes stood still realising there was no point in chasing the shot. Not Greg. He raced down the pitch and took off after the ball. Only a restraining arm stopped a mad dash to the fence.

The incident reminded Roebuck of the enthusiasm shown in kids' games where the bowler bowls with a tennis ball, then fields his own deliveries and the wicket is a garbage can.

The public have responded to the image the writers portray. People from all walks of life and all generations respond positively to Greg. In a survey of 25,000 young people, 90 per cent of them nominated Greg as their favourite sporting personality. Allan Border came in second. Rex Mossop, the veteran Sydney sports commentator, said of Greg: 'He makes you proud to be an Australian.'

Old cricketers have written to Greg saying the game was dead before he came along. Old people tell him he has given them something to look forward to. Very young women write saying they love him and he is a real spunk. Drunks slap him on the back and want to be his mate. People from New Zealand have sent him gifts saying they wanted him to have something nice to remember their country by. The Test fast bowler Dave Gilbert, whom Greg calls Lizard, said whenever he went out socially with him all sorts of people would come up to Greg and say 'Thank you for entertaining us.'

When I told a great-aunt I was writing about Greg she said: 'He's got a lot of life, the rest of the team is dead . . . I sit up and watch him whenever he comes on the TV.'

Her husband said, 'He certainly is a character and bloody good cricketer.'

Greg is a hero to those who want to be a successful part of a team, company or social group, recognised by the establishment, yet very much their own person. Rebels with conservative causes. Greg Matthews proves you don't have to be a clone to make it and many people love him for it. His wacky personality entertains.

But it is not quite cricket to some. So it is not surprising that not everyone in that world has taken so kindly to Greg. Many players and followers of the game think he is decidedly strange. He offends many people's sense of how cricket should be played and who should play it. Emotion should be suppressed on the field. Anything more demonstrative than removing one's hands from the hips after the taking of a wicket is a bit much.

He riles the most conservative groups. He was very unpopular in New Zealand where spectators carried anti-Matthews banners. A group of cricketer followers from Quirindi said, 'There is one bloke we all can't stand and that is Greg Matthews. We hate the way he carries on. Those antics of his are just a disgrace.' Former great, Neil Harvey, wrote that some of his mates refused to watch Greg on television.

'There is nothing of the traditional cricketer in his behaviour,' one first grade cricketer said, 'I find some of things he does offensive. Traditionalists can't relate to him.'

He was not a popular junior cricketer. He was a master sledger and put many of his opponents off him forever. Michael Snell, who played with and against Greg as a schoolboy, said, 'If we had to have a personality cricketer, why does it have to be someone like Greg Matthews.'

When Greg initially hit the first class scene the established cricketers did not take to him at all. Dirk Wellham, a long standing admirer of Greg's, said, 'He got on people's nerves a bit, but was always regarded as a good cricketer . . . Some people found him hard to take.'

Some still do. One Sydney first grade player said: 'You would not give him the time of day if he were not such a good cricketer. Imagine if you had to work with him.'

An old teammate from Cumberland, Bob Aitken, said diplomatically, 'He is certainly one of a kind.' Even his supporters have their reservations. Bill O'Reilly said, 'He is a bit of a weirdo . . . He's a one off-er . . . life is not always easy for the one off-er.' His mother said, 'Greg is just different.'

Some find Matthews' dress offensive. His clothes don't fall into any set category. The back pages of the newspapers referred to him as a punk rocker with a radical mohican hair style. Yet if Greg went out for a night in Sydney no one would look at him twice, unless they thought some of his clothes a bit garish.

Greg cannot understand the fuss. 'I think the press just played it up. I don't paint my face or dye my hair, wear glue in it or any such stuff even though I used to have very short hair, making it look spikey so it stood on end. Maybe I wear clothes slightly different from others but nothing like what I think a punk would wear.'

What about the spiked hair?

'It was my mother. She used to tell me if I kept my hair short it would remain strong and last longer'.

When Greg was 14 and long hair was in he used to wear his to the shoulders. A fight ensued.

'Greg get your hair cut.' Neita would say.

'No Mumma.'

'Get your hair cut.'

'No Mumma.' Greg won the battle because it was his hair, but it seems that Neita won the war.

Many people are put off by his confidence which borders on arrogance. Greg never hesitates when it comes to offering advice. He lives very much in the present. If he thinks something he will say it. He is not one to dwell on the ramifications of his actions. There is no censoring mechanism between brain and mouth. If it feels right it comes out.

Greg once decided to give Rodney Hogg a spot of advice. Hogg was not in the slightest bit interested and let Greg know it without sparing his feelings.

Matthews' advice-giving is not restricted to cricket. When I first met him I told him I did not really have a clear idea of what the book would be like. He said: 'I don't mean to tell you your job or anything, but if I were doing the book I would work out the first ten paragraphs, then the next ten and so on.' Right. I knew how Hogg felt.

I later told him the reason people may think him arrogant is that he is so opinionated and confident. I reminded him of our earlier conversation when he advised me about writing this book. 'Did I give that impression? I don't feel it. Maybe it is just my tone. It just popped into my head if I was writing a book it would have blah, blah, blah in it. Your statement was that you did not have blah blah blah blah together. I thought it might help, so I told you.'

Greg has an interest in people and does his best to make them happy. When the mother of Dave Gilbert, the NSW and Australian fast bowler, was very ill in hospital, Greg was in a telethon.

He gave Mrs Gilbert a cheerio and get-well call. It made her day. People in the hospital came up to her and asked her how she and her son were going. It brightened the last three weeks of her life.

Greg asked me if I had spoken to his father, who seems to have received little attention through Greg's success. I told him I had and he was pleased.

Greg is very conscious of doing the right thing by young people. Phil Derriman, a sometime elegant cricket writer for the *Sydney Morning Herald*, arranged for his 14-year-old nephew to have some batting practice with Bob Holland, the likeable NSW and Australian off-spinner. When Derriman arrived at the training session at the Sydney Cricket Ground he could not see Holland anywhere. He spotted Greg, explained the situation and asked him if he knew where Holland was.

'I don't know', Greg said, 'But I will give him a bat.'

He advised the young man to develop the art of spin bowling. 'There are a million seamers in the world', Greg said, 'and they are all the same.'

When Greg signs autographs he gets the kids to form an orderly line and wait in turn. Once a mature woman attempted to jump the queue to get an autograph.

'I am more than happy to sign an autograph for you', Greg said to her. 'But you will have to line up like everyone else.' She smiled, went to the end of the line, waited and got her autograph.

Greg feels he relates to people of all types. He has enjoyed a cup of tea with Stork Henry, the oldest living Test cricketer, and hopes to have the chance to catch up with him and 'his good lady Violet', again soon. He also considers Jillian's young niece a friend.

Greg won over Dennis Moore, who works with Bob Simpson, the former captain and current Cricket Manager of the Australian team, who manages Greg's business affairs. Moore has a picture of his grandchildren on his desk and Greg regularly asks how they are going. 'He is a tremendous bloke. There are not too many people who think about things like that. He really thinks of the kiddies', Moore said.

Greg respects his elders and calls people he meets for the first time either Mr or Mrs because it sounds right. Yet you could imagine him saying to a venerable old cricketer, 'Hey man. I'm stoked to meet you . . . I really enjoyed rapping to you. I'll catch you later.' He refers to the revered English cricket writer, John Arlott as Johnnie.

How did the young guy from the Western Suburbs of Sydney become such a walking bundle of contradictions. How did he manage to capture the imagination of so many? What created his incredible self-confidence?

The man who did much to create Greg Matthews the enigmatic public personality and Test cricket player died shortly before Greg played his first Test. Gordon Nolan was more than a second father to Greg.

Peter Neita and Greg, Wallsend 1964

YOUNG CRICKETERS WANTED

Greg was eight and big brother Peter was nine when the Matthews' family loaded up their belongings and moved from Newcastle to West Ryde in Sydney. Shortly after the move Greg's mum, Neita, was shopping when she saw a sign which read, 'Young cricketers wanted. Phone Gordon Nolan.' The Matthews family had been involved in cricket for a long time. The boys father, Neville, had been president of the Wallsend cricket club in Newcastle where he played representative cricket and bowled off-breaks. Neita thought it would be a good idea if her boys joined a club. So she took Greg and Peter to practice at nearby Upjohn Park which was to become a second home to them.

Greg's memories of those days are a fuzzy blur. But Neita can remember him as a miniature soccer player. 'Even as a little fellow he was very tenacious. As a three-year-old soccer player he would score ten goals a season. I can remember in one game in the under-fives he got the ball down at one end and dribbled it up to the other end to score. I had tears running down my cheeks. I can still remember the look of determination on his face.'

Neita Matthews is an all-Australian netball umpire, the co-ordinator of the NSW Netball Association executive and a senior vice-president of the Eastwood-Ryde Netball Association.

She umpired at the inaugural South Pacific Games in Fiji in 1978 and has travelled extensively in the South Pacific and Sri Lanka for netball. Brother Peter said Greg inherited his fierce competitiveness and determination from Neita. Some of her old netball rivals never forgave her for her competitive deeds. 'They used to say, "He is Neita Matthews boy" ', she said, 'now they say, "She is Greg Matthews mother." '.

Neita Matthews, Australian netball umpire

Greg was an outstanding schoolboy sportsman. He played representative Rugby League and Union as a schoolboy, won prizes for golf and tennis and was an outstanding soccer player. He played for the CHS cricket team for three years.

Considering Greg's array of sporting skills it is ironic that it was brother Peter who was first tipped by the experts of the day to be the player of the future. They said he had the solid temperament to make it to the top, whereas Greg was the flashy but iffy player who could not be relied on. Peter's future in cricket ended when he became immersed in the world of marine insurance and went to England to further his career.

Anyway Peter was not one to trust experts. He knew from an early age that he would never be as good as Greg. 'I did not want it enough', Peter said. 'Greg always had that something extra that all great players have . . . They all have a certain quality about them . . . I thought I was doing well if I took seven wickets and scored 50 runs. Greg would think he was doing well if he got a 100 runs and 15 wickets. The cream rises to the top pretty quickly at that level . . . Making it to the very top has more to do with attitude than anything else . . . Greg always had that extra drive, that hunger for it . . . I did not want to be that good.'

Many players had the talent but not the attitude. Rick Allen, who later become the cricket writer for the Sydney *Sun*, had more than enough talent to play for Australia. According to Peter, he showed more promise than Dirk Wellham or Greg in the juniors, did enough to be selected for the Australian under-19 team, but did not want success badly enough to make it any further and fell by the wayside. 'He was a great talent', Peter said.

Greg had the drive and the tenacity even in the backyard Tests against brother Peter. Peter would often bat first, get a few runs, then Greg would bat and score a bundle. Peter would return for his second innings and be bowled cheaply again. When Peter said, 'You don't need to bat again. You've already won', Greg would insist. He needed the practice. The one-sided Test match would resume in earnest. Greg's competitiveness would bring out the fire in Peter who would then do anything in his power to get his aggressive

Wallsend RSL soccer club, 1966. Peter is standing on left of the tall boy. Greg is sitting on the far left of the bench.

younger brother's wicket. Greg would be pleased with the effect he had on his brother because it gave him better practice.

Greg, while aggressive by nature is not a big man. He stands 173.5 centimetres tall and weighs 73 kilograms. When he was young he was always small for his age. He did not really shoot up until his late teens. When he was an eight-year-old in the under-elevens, he was tiny. Greg was selected to play in the A. B. Green Shield when he was eleven. The team were supposed to wear long trousers. There were none small enough for Greg so he had to play his aggressive brand of cricket in shorts and long white socks.

The boys began playing in the under-elevens as eight-and-nine-year-olds. The coaches used to put little Greg out of harm's way on the boundary. If the ball came near him he would scurry after it and then desperately try and hurl it back. He did not have the strength to get it to the keeper on the full and became horribly frustrated. He hated to fail at anything even as an eight-year-old.

Gordon Nolan became the coach of the under elevens when Greg was nine. Neville Matthews, Greg's dad, worked on Saturday and was unable to become as closely involved with Greg's cricketing career as he would have liked. Mr Nolan was to fill that role. He would do much to mould Greg Matthews into the player and competitor he is today.

Mr Nolan worked as an accountant for Price Waterhouse then had a managerial position with Otis Elevators, but he was not materialistic and lived in a fibro house in the Western Suburbs. He was a strong Labor man who believed in the value of hard work. His interest in politics never rubbed off on Greg. Outside his work and cricket his major interest was tending the grounds and flower beds at Upjohn Park, an interest that did rub off on Greg.

His death two months before Greg's Test debut added more than a touch of sadness to the event. Shortly after Mr Nolan's death, Greg said, 'Nr Nolan always said he would come and watch me play my first Test no matter where it was. It will take a lot of gloss off the fact if I do play Test cricket one day, he will not be there to watch it . . . I really miss him. What I do now is for me. But I felt tremendous pleasure out of the fact that he enjoyed my being successful.'

51

In his First Test against Pakistan at the Melbourne Cricket Ground, Greg was in his 60's when his thoughts turned to Mr Nolan, whom he always refers to as Mr Nolan. He began to think of how he could publicly pay tribute to his mentor for the contribution he had made in producing Greg Matthews, the Test cricketer. He set his heart on scoring a century in Mr Nolan's honour. He began to plan that, when he reached 100, he would walk to the middle of the pitch, bow his head and have a minutes silence for Mr Nolan. 'Think of the publicity he would have got', Gary Oakes, one of Greg's oldest friends, said. 'But he was quite sincere about it. I know he would have done it.' Greg's sense of timing can be perfect. The stage was set. But even the greatest stage manager needs a bit of luck and Greg did not get it. He was given leg-before-wicket for 75. He felt he had hit the ball, was more than doubly disappointed at what he thought was a wrongful decision and reacted accordingly by punching his bat and mouthing at the umpire. But more of that later.

Greg would have his chance to pay homage in an interview shortly after Mr Nolan's death. 'He was everything to me. He made me what I am cricket-wise. My ways, my attitude, my aggression, are all due to him . . . He taught me so much. To show aggression when you bat. To be aggressive when you bowl. To bowl for wickets and not maidens. He made me what I am. He gave me drive – everything.'

Mr Nolan knew Greg better than anyone. He could look at Greg play for ten minutes and then say, 'You are doing this and this wrong.' Greg had more faith in Mr Nolan than anyone else in his cricket life. He was the only person Greg would really listen to. Nine times out of ten he would heed Mr Nolan's advice and bang – everything would fall into place. 'I really miss that', Greg said. 'He is the most knowledgeable man I have known. If he were alive today [1986] I would be a better cricketer.'

Luckily for Greg, Bob Simpson came along. The first time they met was at a training session for the Western Suburbs club. Simpson noticed the effervescent Greg immediately. But Greg was a little more circumspect. 'Of course it was nice to meet Bob Simpson, the ex-great, and I was Greg Matthews, just another cricketer. There were a hundred other guys just like me there. The meeting was no big occasion.'

But when Simpson was coaching a NSW team which included Greg, 'Simmo' was impressed. 'This bloke has really got it', he thought. It was the opinion of an expert not shared by many. Even though Greg had played five Tests, he was always the player called in when someone was not playing well. Something was not quite clicking sufficiently well enough to make Greg a regular. Simpson saw the potential. 'I think a lot of people laughed at me', Simpson said, 'but I saw a certain quality in him.'

Simpson is a self-confessed traditionalist. Greg is the most outrageous cricketer in the country, yet they respect each other. Simpson said he and Greg hit it off the moment they met. Greg's enthusiasm and love for the game won Simpson over immediately. The fact that they had something in common would not have hurt. Simpson captained Australia from 1963 to 1968, retired, then came out of retirement in 1977-78 to captain Australia when World Series cricket began and led Australia to victory against India.

When Simpson first became closely associated with Greg he was impressed with the solid foundations which Mr Nolan had helped lay. Simpson was able to bring his knowledge and expertise to Greg and refine his technique even further. But perhaps his greatest contribution was his support and encouragement, something Greg badly needed when he broke into Test cricket. He had been used to incessant positive feed back from Mr Nolan all his life and, when he needed it most, it was not there. Although Greg broke into Test cricket with a flourish, he failed to consolidate his position and was written off by many a critic. There was no-one to keep the good positive words flowing and Greg struggled. When he returned from an unsatisfying tour of England with the Australian team, Simpson was there to give him positive strokes and good advice.

At that stage Greg was forgetting the strengths which had got him there in the first place. He was trying to play like Viv Richards, not himself. 'He was trying to hit the cover off the ball. In other words, he was trying perhaps to hit the ball too hard and I said, "Hang on, mate,

Bob Simpson and Greg Matthews

that's not your strength. You're great between wickets, you run like the wind, you're a good mover of the ball. Do your own thing, don't try to be someone else." In other words put pressure on the opposition with your hustling.' It is a very effective tactic. When we were sidetracked during an interview for this book, Greg would say, 'Right next question . . . Remember I have to be out of here by four o'clock.' Right where were we.

Neita Matthews said Simpson was far more easy-going than Mr Nolan, who treated cricket practice as a religious exercise. He was very definite about his views and exacting on Greg. Like all good preachers Mr Nolan demanded the best but was always willing to show the way. A black-and-white view of the world can be useful in sport, where self-doubt is a killer.

Mr Nolan was a hard man, yet Greg never felt physically threatened by him. Mr Nolan expected a lot from everyone. He told Greg how one of his employees had come to him asking for a raise.

'Why do you deserve a raise', Mr Nolan asked.

'Because I work hard', the employee replied.

'What are you paid to do?' Mr Nolan asked. The employee walked out raiseless.

Mr Nolan was very much the traditionalist when it came to cricket and Greg could relate. 'Mr Nolan was very much in the old vein in that things were always better in the past, and society had changed a lot. I tend to agree with that. There are a lot of gimmicks in the game now, which is part of it – electronic scoreboards, coloured clothes, things like that. The game has definitely changed, and he was more in favour of the old style of play. Gentlemenly conduct. He was not into sledging – just the aggression of being able to stand on your own two feet and back your own ability.'

There were many other boys as talented as Greg, but Mr Nolan was drawn by Greg's enthusiasm and willingness to work hard, which he considered the most valuable of qualities. Neita remembers many brilliant young players who failed to apply themselves like Greg and fell by the wayside. Nothing even looked like distracting Greg. He would put his heart and soul into cricket no matter what. One time

Neita drove up to Curtis Oval at Dundas where Greg's under-14 team were playing. Greg's team were in the field. Neita could count only seven players on the field. It was a vital match for Rydalmere. They needed to win outright to get into the finals. For one reason or another they were short and the opponents would not lend them an extra fieldsman. It was about 100 degrees and the young chaps threw themselves around the ground as though the fate of the universe hung on the result. At the end of the hot day they failed by two wickets to win outright.

The intensity young Greg brought to his cricket would put many Test players to shame. After a string of outs Greg's whole world would turn grey. Fifteen years down the track he can remember the pain of failure. 'I don't know where the passion came from', he said. 'But I was always pretty intense about cricket. I can remember when I was eleven I had a duck, a three and another duck. It shot my averages about terribly, but more importantly I was not getting runs. I was terribly upset . . . I sometimes think if only I had that commitment these days.' His mother remembers just how grim her Greg was during a run of outs.

But one area of his play that has never let him down is his fielding. One of Mr Nolan's requirements was that Greg be a good fielder – the logic being that he could save 20 or 30 runs an innings through sound fielding and earn his place in the team when all else failed, as it must at some stage. Today Greg's fielding is an inspiration for teammates and a delight for spectators to cheer.

Simpson said Greg's batting was technically very correct. Greg had a very good eye and could pick a ball's line and length very well. He could tell which ball was there to be punished and which was the one to leave.

According to Bob Simpson, players such as Wayne Phillips, Greg Ritchie and David Boon were more naturally gifted than Greg, but Greg has made the most of what he has got by working hard on his game over the years, refining his technique, eliminating errors. It pays off. The fewer faults a batsman has the fewer times he will get out and the more runs he will make. A sound technique must bear the test of time. The second year in Shield cricket is normally harder than the first. If a player has any weaknesses they will be exposed in the first season and exploited in the second, sometimes fatally. Greg's second season of Shield cricket was better than his first and he has improved every year since.

The South African born opener, Keppler Wessels, is a classic example of a player who was worked out by his opponents. When he first came to Australia he was a sensation in the Sheffield Shield competition for Queensland. Shortly after he was naturalised and made eligible for Australia. He played some outstanding Test innings, but the bowlers discovered he had a weakness if the ball was pitched around leg stump. He had a horrible run of outs, battled to rectify the fault and after much angst partially succeeded.

Simpson says that sometimes Greg gets over-excited when he bats, can get carried away, can try to force the play when it is inappropriate and wind up getting himself out in the process. Greg prefers not to dwell publicly on his batting weaknesses. If he has any the bowlers can do their best to find them out.

Greg is a great deflector of the ball, he dabs it past point particularly well. He is an accumulater of runs rather than a player who takes an attack apart. You can be watching him play and think everything is plodding along nicely, when you suddenly realise he is on 50 or 60. His most spectacular shot is the on-drive, one of Greg Chappell's prettiest. His strong personality makes it extremely difficult for bowlers to intimidate him.

Greg's bowling is less advanced than his batting, partly because he finds batting the more fascinating. But mainly because spin bowling is a very exact art/science which takes years to get anywhere near perfect. Simpson says Greg has a very natural action and lets the ball go easily and smoothly. Bill O'Reilly is impressed. 'His bowling is forceful, persistent and technically 100 per cent correct and reliable.'

Greg thinks his bowling will get better and better. In early 1986 he said, 'I have only been bowling for the last four to five years. I am still very raw. There are still a few things I want to do to my bowling action. I just need to hold my batting position and perhaps I shall be looked on as the fifth bowler – somewhat like Richie Benaud. I'm just in awe to mention his name. I understand that when he first started playing it took him a while to become a front-line bowler in Test cricket. Not that I believe I shall take 248 Test wickets, but I would like to think I could become a more important part of the attack.'

Simpson thinks that Greg needs to develop patience in his bowling and plan how he is going to get a batsman out. At the moment Greg trys to get the batsman out with every ball. But even the experts disagree. Bill O'Reilly, who was taken with Greg's bowling the first time he saw him play, said when he bowled he always tried to get the batsman out with every ball he bowled and thought this was a good practice for any spinner.

Even though it was as a batsman that Greg became recognised as a valuable Test player, it was his spin bowling which initially enabled him to get into the Australian team. Just before the First Test team for the match against Pakistan was announced in 1983, Phil Derriman wrote in the *Sydney Morning Herald*, 'These days a promising Sheffield Shield batsman could peel off a string of centuries and still find five or six others queuing ahead of him for a place in the Test side. If he is a spin bowler, a dash of talent could speed him to the head of the queue.'

Ever since the retirement of Gary Gilmour in 1977, the Australian selectors have been anxious to find an all-rounder to give the team more balance. There were few candidates around when the Fourth Test was chosen and Greg was given his chance – many said prematurely. Greg was picked primarily on the strength of his bowling but he had not really started bowling regularly in first grade until half-way through 1981 when he moved from Cumberland to Wests. Two years later he is talking about consolidating his position as a batsman and maybe being the fifth bowler.

Surprise, surprise. It was Mr Nolan who first told Greg to become a spin bowler. During his early junior years Greg used to bowl spin and pace. Pace bowlers in the Dennis Lillee, Jeff Thomson mould were the rage and most young cricketers wanted to emulate them.

But Mr Nolan told Greg he did not have the build to become an out-standing pace bowler so he was better off sticking to spin. Besides, pace bowlers were a dime a dozen and there was a shortage of good spin bowlers. Mr Nolan told Greg to learn the craft while he was young so he would have a very useful asset for later life. When Greg went to play grade cricket he was given few bowling opportunities and was told to concentrate on batting. But Mr Nolan urged Greg to keep working on his bowling in the nets.

Greg's father, Neville, was of the same persuasion. When Greg was picked to play representative cricket in Wagga as a young teenager, his father said, 'Now Greg don't forget to bowl your slowies. Everyone is bowling fast, but you remember your slowies.' Greg bowled his slowies, took a bag of wickets and came back triumphant. He had been selected for the NSW Primary Schools team and named captain.

Mr Nolan's contribution went beyond the laying of a sound technical framework and giving sound advice. He never doubted Greg's ability. He was always telling Greg, 'One day you will wear the green and gold. One day. One day . . . You will wear the baggy green cap one day. I know it . . . One day.' The confidence and encouragement were priceless to any cricketer, particularly one with Greg's drive and determination. If the mountain is defined and someone you respect says you can climb it, the work does not seem in vain.

And Greg had great faith in Mr Nolan. When Greg was in his late teens he tried to encourage Gary Oakes to work harder on his cricket. 'Come on Oaksie you can do it', he would say. 'Mr Nolan says you are good enough . . . Come on let's hustle.' Mr Nolan said Oaksie could do it, but Oaksie did not get the message, or maybe he just never had the will. Oaksie played first grade at 18 and had three trials with the NSW team, but never went beyond that. 'I did not set my goals high enough', Oaksie said. When he looks at some of the fast bowlers who have played Test cricket there is more than a trace of sadness in his voice. No athlete feels more pain than those who might have been and there are plenty of them.

If Greg and/or Mr Nolan decided a young player was not up to the mark, Greg would have no hesitation in letting him know. Greg was not always supportive. One day Greg was practising at Upjohn Park with Oaksie and the best player in another age group called Geoff who opened the batting and bowling for his team. Greg was batting. When Oaksie bowled Greg just blocked the balls away. But when Geoff bowled Greg smashed him all over the park. Geoff was not amused. He asked Greg what was going on.

'You are no good', Greg said. 'You have got no talent, you might as well give up cricket now. I don't want you to bowl to me.' Greg and Mr Nolan did not think Geoff had what it took to be a good cricketer. I asked Greg why he did not like Geoff. 'I have got nothing against him as a person', he said. 'I never thought he was much of a player and I was proved right he never got into first grade even though he was supposed to be a big star ... I never treated him badly as a human being. I was just pointing out I was better, as he was a challenger for my place as number one junior at Rydalmere.'

Even though some would disagree, Mr Nolan did not breed the over-confidence which can be deadly. Mr Nolan told Greg he was good enough but only if he put in the work. He would have to do this and that to get there. It was never going to be easy, he would have to work, but he could do it. There is a difference between arrogance and over-confidence. Mr Nolan made sure that Greg knew his faults. He would analyse the how and the why of each of Greg's dismissals and then show him where he had gone wrong. He asked a great deal but he gave more. He helped many young people, but Greg was special.

Through Mr Nolan Greg developed that trait sport psychologists refer to as coachability. All that means is that players are able to absorb the good advice that they are given. As in matters of the heart good advice is often only what you agree with. But being able to act on advice is easier said than done, just ask Andrew Hilditch. During the summer of 1985 everyone vaguely interested in cricket realised that Hilditch should not hook. As Frank Keating said of Hilditch, 'Short! Hook! Fine Leg's! Thanks!' That was in England. Hilditch returned home, was picked for the First Test against New Zealand, and was once again out hooking.

Bob Simpson said it was important to do the right kind of practice. Ian Chappell said he could derive more benefit from a two hours' practice than Hilditch would from two-weeks worth. Mr Nolan taught Greg to always question advice and to ask how and why something should be done and if it made sense to adjust his game accordingly. Simpson has found Greg to be an excellent student of the game who puts into practice the advice he agrees with.

Greg and Mr Nolan's conversations were not restricted to cricket. Many of the Nolan values have been solidly instilled in Greg. They met when Greg was eight, saw each other regularly when he was nine and began practicing regularly with him from the age of ten. They spoke about everything.

'He had a great effect on me', Greg said. 'My mother says she sees a lot of things that he had said come out of me. I am very proud of that because he was a great man.'

How so?

'He was honest, trustworthy, straightforward, loyal, spoke his mind, was generous to his friends, believed that true wealth came not from material possessions but knowledge and he worked as hard as anyone I have seen. I guess that covers him in fair detail.'

And you have inherited these qualities?

'I'd like to think so though I would not have any particular reason to say it. It's just that I try to be aware of my responsibilities as a human being and as a cricketer.'

While no-one would describe Greg as a saint, Mr Nolan and his ideas have a strong hold. Greg has even passed them on to Jillian. Sometimes she even says, 'I wonder what Mr Nolan would have thought of this.'

Greg learnt the value of good positive vibrations from Mr Nolan and it lifts Greg's teammates. But more importantly the constant postive feedback Mr Nolan emitted gave Greg confidence in his own ability. So whenever he has been in a sticky squeeze he has had the confidence to play his natural game and, when he failed, to fight his way back.

When Greg was dropped after a disastrous Test against the West Indies many said it was the end of the road. 'I knew I was good enough', Greg said. 'I had scored runs in a Test against Pakistan, they may not have had the greatest attack . . . but I had done it once and there is no reason why I could not do it again. I just went back to Shield cricket and worked on my game.'

Many players never really believe they are good enough to represent their country. They might score prolifically in State cricket only to fail when given their chance in a Test match. More often than not they fail for reasons other than poor technique. Often the occasion proves too big for the player's character. Stephen Waugh, the NSW batsman whose natural talent Greg is very impressed with, struggled during his first Tests because he was incredibly nervous.

From Mr Nolan Greg evolved the self-confidence and mental equipment to handle pressure. A maiden Test is enough to test the nerves of Batman. So when Greg got his chance against Pakistan after only a handful of Shield games, you would expect him to be tentative.

He had good reason to be unsure of himself. Many doubted Greg's effectiveness, particularly as a Test spin bowler. He had only taken 23 first class wickets, the MCG wicket was dead and Greg has never liked bowling there. Yet in his first test he felt relaxed enough to sweep the spinner, Abdul Quadir, early on in his innings and was sufficently composed to score 75 runs and take four wickets.

Most players freeze up when they reach 90. Greg can handle those character-testing nineties without any problem. He plays each ball on its merits regardless of the situation and reached his first Test century with a six.

It was not just the positive talk from Mr Nolan which made Matthews such a confident, self-assured character. Mr Nolan believed in Greg and his actions spoke as loudly as his words. Greg was always the automatic captain, and always the best player.

The world seemed to revolve around making Greg the best possible cricketer he could be. Mr Nolan and Greg would practice and talk about his game for hours. Mr Nolan would tell Greg what he was doing wrong, as well as the why and the how. When you know the how and the why, you should know when to do what to whom.

All of which goes a long way to understanding the older Greg. It is not that Greg does not think other people's time is valuable, it's just that it is not as valuable as his. It can be annoying. Dave Gilbert and two other friends were playing golf. It was a ladies day and they were allowed to tee off at the tenth to miss the congestion. Just as they were about to tee off, Greg said, 'I have just got to go and make a few phone calls.' Greg disappeared with his diary. It was pretty tense stuff. The women golfers were charging up the course. Gilbert and his friends studied the boards with past champions written on them. It was touch and go whether they would be stuck behind a slow group of older women or have a clear run. Where is Greg?

Twenty-five minutes after they arrived Greg reappeared ready to play. 'You would not tolerate it in anyone else but Greg. He seems to get away with it. I know when I pick him up I will be waiting for 20 minutes. I would not dare be late.' Oaksie says Greg hates other people doing what he does himself. It is quite a sin to waste Greg's time.

If you want to see Greg he consults his diary and says, 'Mondays out. Tuesdays out. Wednesdays out . . . ' Oaksie said, 'Sometimes the reason Greg says a day is out is because he wants to sleep that day. It's what he wants to do so he does it. Everyone has to fit in.'

Once Oaksie had not seen Greg for eleven months. He rang up. Greg answered the phone.

'Gary Oakes here.'

'Oaksie, Oaksie, great to hear from you. Look I am in the middle of dinner now I will call you back.' He rang back an hour later. It sounded reasonable to Oaksie but he thought if the roles had been reversed he would have behaved differently.

When they finally got to see each other it was at the SCG near the press box. Howard Northey, a journalist who Greg deems a friend, was also there. Greg wanted to focus in on Oaksie. He turned to Northey and said, 'I have not seen my man Oaksie for ages. Howie why don't you go buy yourself a drink.'

One time Greg got Gilbert to stop the car he was driving so Greg could get a special lighter out of the boot to light a cigarette. Greg expects a great deal. Often when he visited Oaksie at home, he would walk into the bathroom and ask to use his toothbrush. 'Greg does things to you that you would never dream of doing to him', Oaksie said. 'But that's Greg and I still love him.'

Greg's rise to stardom was incredibly rapid yet he has handled it as though it was quite natural. After all he had been the star of his own world since he was ten. He has a support team today. Bob Simpson handles his business affairs. Jillian introduces him to new music and is in charge of food, Greg has not got the time. His mother looks after his mail, filters telephone calls, keeps a press clipping and video file. He introduced me to people as his author.

This egocentricity rubs some people the wrong way. Brother Peter said, 'I was the nice guy and Greg was the bastard. He wasn't really, just very competitive.' Oaksie hated Greg until he got to know him well. 'Sixty guys out of 66 (in a club) would hate Greg', Oaksie said. 'But those six that knew him would love him.' David Gilbert remembers seeing Greg at a junior cricket lunch sitting by himself because no-one else wanted to sit next to him.

Michael Snell, who played with and against Greg as a junior, said 'I knew Greg well enough to know I did not want to know him better. He was always very opinionated ... and had a high opinion of himself. Gordon Nolan told him he was better than anyone else and he believed it. Nolan believed that the solar system emanated in the vicinity of Greggie's backside, I don't know if Nolan called him Greggie, but I always think of him as Greggie.'

Snell remembers captain Greg giving his opening bowler a couple of overs and then taking the ball from him when he did not succeed and bowling himself for 25 overs. He can even recall Greg playing wicket keeper at the start of an under-12 Causey Shield game when the regular wicket keeper was injured, take 3 catches, 2 stumpings and then whipping the gloves off to have a bowl. It would have been outrageous behaviour if he had not been so dedicated and talented a player. Maybe it was anyway. But cricket was Greg's life. He would often play junior cricket in the morning and senior cricket in the afternoon.

Mr Nolan's faith in and concentration on Greg was justified. He was the outstanding player for his team, a cut above the rest and the first picked for the junior representative teams. Some of his junior records still stood in 1986.

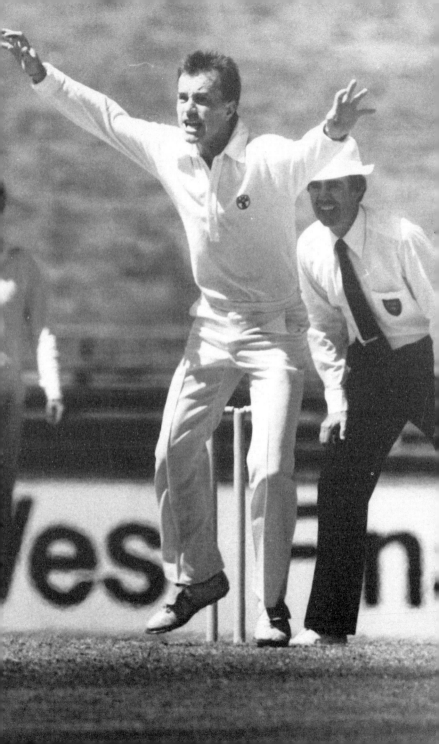

'He was always a class player', Snell said. 'I would have been very surprised if he had not at least reached the level of Shield cricket. He was the wicket you always wanted to get. I remember getting him out and being very happy. He was the man in those days. Everyone looked up to him. He was very good at getting other people to do the right thing.'

It was not only because of his talents as a cricketer that made it such a pleasure for his opponents to get him out. Greg was a liberal sledger as a kid. If a batsman was playing it safe on a treacherous wicket, Greg would start slow hand clapping. And when a batsman played at a ball outside the off stump, got an edge and was caught out, Greg would say, 'Well left sunshine.' To a young batsman playing at a ball and missing, 'Another coat of paint sunshine and we would have had you.'

Even Neita admits that Greg was not always an angel. 'He was like all other brash young men. He thought he could conquer the world. He would go out and think he could thrash someone around and would get out for a duck and the opposing team would be pleased to think that they had got Greg the mighty mouth Matthews out . . . '

Greg was not the easiest person to umpire as a young chap. He would spit the dummy if he was given out to a doubtful decision. If he thought he had been wronged he would let the umpire know exactly what he thought. The umpire would probably be some kid's father who had been roped in for the day and did not really know what he was doing. Greg of course knew the rules inside out.

Snell said, 'If you got him out, you wanted it to be a catch off a full blooded drive or you wanted to see the stumps sprayed all over the ground.'

Greg learned earlier than most that cricket is not just a game. Nolan often picked Greg up to go to games or to practice. They would watch the Tests together and discuss the strengths and weaknesses of the Test players. Greg said it was uncanny the way Mr Nolan could pick when and how a Test player would get out. They brought an intensity to their cricket which was lost on many of the other players and coaches to whom the game was something they did before mowing the lawns on Saturday afternoons. It was nice to win and score runs and a shame to get out, but no worse than when Dr Who was trapped by the Darleks on tele. To Greg and Mr Nolan these games were a thoroughly decent obsession.

Young Greg was a walking encyclopaedia of cricket information. He used to read all the cricket books and magazines and watch all the first class games on television, and whenever possible watch the first grade games. He knew what he wanted to be. The Test players were his role models. If he heard that Doug Walters used to revolve his head when he went out to bat in order to loosen up the neck or to help his eyes adjust to the sun, he would take on the mannerism. At the age of 14 he looked like a Test player.

AN UNLIKELY CAREER PATH

One of the reasons there are so many phenomenal black athletes in the United States is that, for many, sport is the best career path to fame and fortune. If a young black, whose parents have not realised the American dream, is good at American Football the way to go is clear – pump iron, get in the high school team, get noticed by a scout, win a scholarship to a strong university, play well, become an all-American, get drafted by a professional team, become a star, do national beer commercials and live happily ever after on the players pension doing the odd promotion. There are plenty of role models to aspire to.

In Australia sport is an unlikely career path. There is no clearly defined professional sports structure as there is in the US. The successful Australian is a solid professional with a nice home, wife, car, dog and children. You can almost hear the middle class parent saying, 'You have to do something while you are playing sport or you will end up too far behind everyone else when you stop playing. You just can't afford the time to run around Australia playing for your State. Look at Johnny Smith he wears that smart suit, has a company car, is paying off that lovely exhibition home and he is only 25. He did not waste time.'

The upper classes have a different attitude. 'Sport . . . great stuff for a young man, builds character, keeps you out of trouble when you are young and keeps you fit, but there is no future in it as a career. A chap can go and have a season of rugger or cricket at Oxford but there comes a time when you have got to be responsible. Broaden yourself young man. Get into computers.'

Such logic rarely applies out in Sydney's West.

Dirk Wellham who came from the same cricket background as Greg, said: 'You just play cricket, you have very little else in your life, so you play cricket. If you are successful you keep going.'

Wellham is a bright young man who would succeed at anything he turned his hand to. He has had a wide range of jobs and now works for PBL Marketing who promote cricket. Wellham has scored a century in his Test debut against England and captained NSW to Sheffield Shield victories.

Chris Chapman grew up in Vaucluse, one of Sydney's more affluent suburbs, attended a private school, went to the University of New South Wales, studied law, was the associate of the Chief Justice of the High Court, Sir Garfield Barwick, worked for a large legal firm, and became legal manager of Channel 7 in Sydney. Chapman was a talented schoolboy cricketer. He played first grade for his university, where he won a blue and scored many nineties. He was selected for the State squad and considered himself a fringe player. Greg remembers him as, 'The straight bat who scored a million 99s.'

Chapman said of Greg, 'He is a real fighter. Time and time again you see these blokes from the Western Suburbs with this driving will to succeed. It takes so much dedication and singleness of purpose to be a great cricketer. You cannot pursue another career at the same time. It is very hard for guys from the North Shore or the Eastern Suburbs to have that hunger to succeed. I have seen hundreds of guys from those suburbs give the game away.'

Bill O'Reilly put it another way. 'They seem to have some very good lucerne in the Western Suburbs, some very good boys come from there. Some marvellous players have come from the GPS schools over the years. But they have not pulled their weight for quite a while now, must be 30 years . . . Must be a lot of rocky ground out at Vaucluse.'

If Michael Snell had Greg's singleness of purpose and drive he could have been a contender for the NSW team. 'I started playing in those schoolboy days and I was pretty intense then, probably as much as Greg. But I got sidetracked with studies and other things, but that never happened with Greg. He is a living testament to the cliche: 'If you put your head down and work your arse off you can get somewhere.' Snell is now a solicitor who plays social cricket.

Greg comes from a comfortable background. Neville Matthews is manager of the Bonds and Kirby furniture store at Bankstown. Neita and Neville, Matthews' parents, encouraged their children at whatever they did. Peter has a successful career in insurance and younger brother, Ian, is studying law. Greg is a cricketer. All are admired for their talents. Greg is proud of his brothers and says they are very successful.

Each were allowed to do their own thing and encouraged when they flourished in whatever field they chose. Greg became besotted with cricket. The regular vocational guidance tests produced no ideas. He can remember two teachers who turned him on and inspired him. But the strong influences in his life were Gordon Nolan and cricket.

'He never knew what he wanted to be or do to make a career as a young fellow', Neita said. 'At one stage he even took up signwriting lessons. He even took his books to study in England when he first played cricket there. His lack of career worried him a bit. He never worried too much about his studies though, he had too many important things to do, like play sport. Schoolwork was just not one of his favourite subjects . . . It seems to have worked out.'

When he left school he landed a job at Grace Brothers, third floor, lounge and dining. According to Greg it was the biggest and best showroom in the Southern Hemisphere. Greg was the youngest person to get a job there in a long time. 'It was quite a job to get,' Greg said.

Did you like it?

'No I hated it. Some guy was going to show me the furniture business. He quit a week after I got there. It was like something out of *Are you being Served*. There was a good looking guy, not the good looking chick, but all the other characters seemed to be there . . . It was hard yakka.'

Not the most tantalising career path. When his mum ran into a friend, Frank Clark, they discussed Greg's future and he agreed to get in touch with a few people in England to see about the possibility of Greg playing cricket there professionally. He told them about Greg and asked if they were interested. They were.

Meanwhile Tony Greig, the former English captain, arranged for

Greg to have a try out with Sussex. But there was no security there. So he settled on Whitehaven, loaded up his kit, went to England and became a full-time professional cricketer.

But before going to England Greg had to battle his way up the grades in Sydney. 'I remember my first game in the fourths very clearly', Greg said, 'My first game in third grade, my first game in second. I remember them all.'

When he joined Cumberland he was advised either to be a batsman or a bowler. Greg never lost sight of his bowling but concentrated on his batting.

Also in the fourths when Greg made his debut was 'Mr Express', a fast bowler who Greg thought was absolutely the best. He was a huge man in first grade who was just coming back after injury. He had a massively long run up and seemed to bowl at a million miles an hour. Greg expected Express to tear the opponents, Northern Districts, apart. He almost felt sorry for the opposition who had to face him.

But Northern Districts had a guy playing for them called Peter Crawford who, unbeknown to Greg, would play first grade a few weeks later. He smashed the Cumberland speed demon all round Sommerville Oval at Eastwood. 'Jeeesus', Greg thought, 'is this what it's like playing grade.'

Northern Districts scored a zillion runs and Greg batted the following weekend. He was tense and nervous. His side's only hope was a draw. Greg managed to hang in there for a couple of hours with the number eleven.

It seemed like the new kid was going to save the side from defeat. There were only four or five overs to go. Northern Districts brought on a leg spinner who just tossed up a series of long hops and full tosses, the easiest balls to hit in cricket. Greg smashed him for four and thought, 'You beauty, I will get a few runs here.'

Pride cometh before a fall. The bowler sent down a long hop. Greg was already enjoying the four runs before he hit the ball. It went down someone's throat rather than into the fence.

Greg walked off thinking: 'Gee I didn't do too badly. I hung in there for a long time.' He expected something like a pat on the back and a: 'Well done. Pity about that catch.'

The team captain was not so impressed. Greg said: 'He was a hard dude who bowled left-arm orthodox. Elderly gentleman in his mid-forties and he really ripped into me. So did the guy at the other end, Graham Donovan, who I always thought was a bit of a gig. I thought I had done a good job. I hung in there for a while, but I saw that they were getting at and that was a lesson.'

Greg was not particularly well-liked at Cumberland from the word go. He was incredibly confident and arrogant and this rubbed many people up the wrong way, who naturally enough did not think Greg was necessarily a better player or human being than they were.

One day he saw Bob Aitken, the first-grade spinner, bowl a delivery he had not seen before. Naturally he wanted to learn how to do it and so he went up to his fellow club mate to ask him.

'Mr Aitken', Greg said, 'how did you do that?'

'Listen sonny I am not going to teach you. I have been practising for 20 years and I am not going to teach you anything. You will probably end up taking my place.'

Aitken was going to affect Greg's life when they got together. But Greg is not one to dwell on things and he kept practising hard. His talent and diligence were rewarded and he made his way up to third grade. Greg's debut in third grade was against Mosman at Rawson Park. Mosman hit a few runs in their first innings. It rained. Cumberland went into bat. Mosman had a couple of opening bowlers who had come down from the seconds who were pretty quick. The ball was flying everywhere and Cumberland was getting hit all over the place.

Greg walked in to bat. He joined a teacher from the Kings School at Parramatta, Cam Stewart, at the crease. Stewart sensed that he and Greg were on a mission from some sporting god or other. Pain was something to be transcended on the way to a glorious draw. Stewart walked down the wicket to talk to Greg.

'Listen', Stewart said, 'its popping and flying a bit, so just take them on the body.'

'What an idiot', thought Greg.

Stewart batted for four hours. At times during the match he ran a foot outside off-stump, stuck his arm out and got hit. Greg was less heroic but at least as effective. His only wound from battle was a slight graze near his eye. He scored 55.

There was only one umpire. The bowler appeared to throw one delivery at Greg. Greg was furious. It was a full toss and he should have hit if for four. 'I was freaked out', Greg said, 'and this guy was suspended.'

After three games in thirds Greg was promoted to seconds. It seems as though most things Greg is associated with are quite extraordinary. His second grade debut against Bankstown at Bankstown Oval was no exception. Steve Small, who went on to play for NSW with Greg, was in the side. Greg scored a duck or, at most, very few. The side made 113. The opposition went in to bat and were one for about 100 overnight. It was hardly worth turning up you would think. But as the American baseball coach Yogi Berra said: 'It aint over till it's over.' The next day Cumberland got the remaining nine wickets for less than 12 runs and won the match.

While in second grade, Greg lost touch with Gordon Nolan. He did not make the time for Mr Nolan, something he still regrets. But he was a growing teenager who had a lot to see and do and thought he could do it all himself. Even though he lived at home, he was a very social being who had many friends and spent much time at their houses.

Greg had two close friends at the time, Oaksie and Mark Hanigan, 'Hanno'. Greg was the extrovert, Hanno was the good solid bloke and Oaksie was in between. One night they were driving home over the Gladesville bridge at 6 am after quite a night out. Greg was driving. Oaksie had to be at work as a panel beater at 6.30 am and was desperate to get home as soon as possible. Greg stopped on the Gladesville Bridge and said: 'Isn't that a beautiful scene.' As they went past Oaksie's place, he begged them to stop. Hanno said, 'I really need my night's sleep, can you drop me home first Greg.' Oaksie was furious, grabbed the steering wheel and forced the car over to the side of the road and jumped out.

But Greg was good to Oaksie, forever trying to get the best out of him. When they were practising, Greg would say: 'Is that as fast as you can bowl? You aren't even as quick as me. You just have not got it.' It would stir him on to greater efforts and he and Greg would have a more productive practice.

I asked Oaksie if he thought Dave Gilbert would be a regular test player?

'Yes. Greg will hold him in there. He did it for me.' In one Poidevan Shield game, an under-21 competition, Greg was captain. Oaksie had bowled about 30 overs and was exhausted. Oaksie bowled a ball down the leg side and the batsman scored off it.

Greg sidled up to Oaksie and whispered: 'Oaksie. Oaksie. What are you doing. I told you to bowl middle and off. Pick it up. I Neeeed you.'

Nevertheless Greg has had his bad patches. At one stage nothing seemed to be going right. His timing was off. The harder he tried the worse it got. When all seemed lost in the civilised world as Greg knew it, he saw Mr Nolan and had a 15 minute session with him. Mr Nolan made two statements to Greg. One was about his cover drive. The other about working the ball off his body. It made sense to Greg and all of a sudden he was having the best streak of his career. In the next three games he made fifties. The week after that he was in first grade.

His first first grade game was against Randwick at the old Kings School. Spectators at grade games are a rare species and there is little publicity.

Was Greg nervous?

'Oh yeah that was big time stuff. It's all relative. If the junior cricket was washed out when I was playing then I would watch first grade. It was the pinnacle. The buzz to watch. It seemed different and better cricket.'

He was 17-years-old and not that well prepared. He felt overawed at the time and did not do very well. He scored six. The one-time Australian opener, John Dyson, dropped him off the bowling of Tim Towers, a pace bowler and son of the legendary Rugby Union player Cyril. Towers cannot remember having played against Greg. Greg, with his extraordinary memory for things cricket, remembers Towers well.

Greg was as keen as ever. This time his over-enthusiasm got him into trouble. Mick O'Haire was bowling to Dyson who hit the ball into the covers. Greg fielded the ball and threw it at the stumps. It went for four overthrows. O'Haire was furious.

Greg may have been young and raw, but he was full of confidence. Greg used to try and goad the bowlers so they would try incredibly hard to get him out, bowl a loose delivery, become frustrated and subsequently have a picnic. One time Greg was playing against David 'Cracker' Hourn the slow bowler from Waverley. Hourn had played for his State the previous week and taken nine wickets for NSW. Greg hit his first ball for four and said: 'How the hell did you get nine wickets?'

Greg would get the opposing bowlers so mad they would clench the ball in whitened knuckles. He used the same strategy as a bowler. He would rubbish a batsman, who would become furious, try and smack Greg around the ground and invariably wind up getting out. Oaksie knew what it was like to fall for the sledging trick. Once he was bowling to Wayne Seabrook, who later played for NSW. Seabrook said: 'How did you manage to hold your place in the team? You are hopeless.' Oaksie picked up his pace and Seabrook was beaten by one ball and got an inside edge, the ball just missed the stumps and fell short of the keeper. After that Oaksie was a beaten man and Seabrook got the better of him. 'I knew I would only have one chance. Greg nearly always got the better of those encounters.'

Once he got in first grade, Greg was never dropped. But at Cumberland he never really looked like breaking through. It did not stop the hurt when someone from Northern Districts was quoted in a magazine as saying that he thought Greg would one day play Shield cricket but never for Australia.

Greg was still playing Rugby for the Eastwood colts. The team had tremendous team spirit – the only side Greg was associated with to have more was the NSW Sheffield Shield team. Eastwood won the grand final 9-0 against Gordon, with Greg, the team's fullback and goal kicker, scoring all the points. Greg still holds a point scoring record of 300 for the Eastwood colts.

Greg's mother remembers the final. 'Greg was a marked man, they gave him hell. They kicked him. They thrashed into him and they

School match at Marsden High School, 1969

knocked into him. He came out all bloody, but he stayed on there and they won. Greg scored all the points and they carried him halfway off the field.'

The next cricket season Greg was picked in first grade against the University of New South Wales. They had the two State fast bowlers in the team, Geoff Lawson and Graham Watson. Greg thought, 'Jeeesus, I will never cut this.' Doug Walters was playing for Cumberland. Greg remembers the game well. 'No disrespect to the man at all but we each scored 45. I got caught down the leg side which is a pretty outrageous way to get out. It was off Mark Ray. Dougie was dropped five times. Easy catches. I faced Lawson for 56 consecutive balls. I felt really good about that. He hit me in the ribs, cracked a rib . . . bitterly disappointed I did not score a 50 . . . Dougie got two points in the *Herald* best and fairest and I did not get any.'

Facing Lawson and coming through the experience with distinction did much to bolster Greg's confidence.

The going was not so smooth in England. Greg arrived at Whitehaven on the Scottish border in 1980. It was not the most luxurious club in the world. No accommodation had been arranged for him and he ended up living in a caravan with two people and a dog. He was a cut above everyone else as a cricketer. In his first year he scored 800 runs, averaging 48, and took 48 wickets. Greg felt he still had something to prove. He did it the next year scoring 1,523 runs and taking 93 wickets. The club won the competition for the first time in 54 years.

When he returned the following season, Greg was expecting a hero's reception. One person picked him up at the airport and again no accommodation had been arranged. 'It was very tacky. A poorly organised club.' But this time he had Oaksie with him.

Oaksie had a great time but was not too impressed with the cricket. The wickets were bad, the people were offhanded and the standard of play was ordinary. Greg was given a car and during the week he and Oaksie would tour around England.

After a while Oaksie put little effort into his cricket. He would bowl at about three-quarter pace and usually have the figures of about one for 40. In one match they played, the team was all out for

Neville, Peter, Greg and Ian Matthews at Sydney Airport on Greg's
departure for England, 1983

86. Greg had made about 15. The boys had had a big night out. Often they had nights out when there was no cricket on, get home 5 am and sleep in until 3.30 pm. But this day there was a game to play.

Greg walked up to Oaksie and said: 'You and me will open the bowling and I will get more wickets than you.' They opened the bowling and Oaksie's game lifted dramatically.

The crowd was hostile. 'They hated Greg', Oaksie said, 'just like every other club he played against while we were there did. They gave us a very hard time.' There was usually quite a fair crowd and the English-style yobbos would yell out, 'Bloody Australians . . . That's just not cricket'. Greg and Oaksie would bowl bouncers. 'Greg was pretty quick when he wanted to be.'

Oaksie took a wicket. Greg then took a wicket. Oaksie took two Greg took two. Both had three wickets. Greg yelled to the score-keeper, 'How many runs have they got off Oaksie.' Oaksie would do the same. Oaksie ended up with something like five for 18, Greg got five for 17.

One time when they were driving around, Oaksie had had a few drinks and rolled the car. The club wanted to deduct the insurance excess from Greg's pay. Greg was furious and after a fight Greg got his money and the two split.

While Greg was in England, Dirk Wellham wrote to ask if he was interested in playing for Western Suburbs. He outlined the advantages of the move. Dirk and Greg had known each other for years. They had played with and against each other in junior competitions and more recently in the NSW Colts team which Dirk had captained.

It was in a Colts match that Dirk had given Greg his first chance to really bowl competitively in senior cricket and Greg went on to take five for 44 off 32 overs during the carnival. While at Cumberland, Greg's bowling was pretty much restricted to the nets. Bob Aitken was the Cumberland first grade spinner. He had been doing the job forever. He had quite a say in the running of the team and Greg never got a look-in as a bowler.

Greg was attracted to Wests because he liked Wellham, was impressed by the fine facilities and the club's long tradition of producing Test players, and felt that a change would be good for him. So he decided to go.

Greg had not been popular at Cumberland. He said he was put off by the club's internal problems and frustrated by the lack of bowling opportunities. Mr Nolan still encouraged him to persevere with his bowling. However Aitken thought the main reason Greg changed clubs was that he knew it would dramatically improve his chances of being picked in the NSW State team.

Something went right at Wests and all of a sudden his career took off. Greg had three exceptional innings in grade cricket, including a century. He also made one playing for the NSW Colts. Despite this he did not expect to get in the State team. There was only one vacancy and a Randwick player, Peter Clifford, who had scored about 350 runs in three games, was widely expected to get in.

One day Greg was practicing at Upjohn Park, near the family home, when he saw his mother walk over with a piece of paper. She looked pleased but had tears in her eyes and was shaking a bit.

Greg said: 'Have you won the lottery Neit?'

'No', she said. 'It's better than that.'

What could be better than that?

'You are in the State team.'

'Oh'. He had a bit more batting practice, took his kit off and was in his car, stopped at the traffic lights, when it sank in. He rolled down the window and let out a giant hoot and began yelling and screaming. He was in the State team. A real-life first-class cricketer. As the Talking Heads say: 'Nothing could be better than that.'

Before that match Greg had a game of golf with Geoff Lawson and Murray Bennett, whom Greg calls 'Big Buddy' and describes as an excellent human being. Lawson left soon after the golf and Bennett and Greg had a beer.

'There's room for both of us in the team', Bennett said. 'At this stage I probably bowl a bit better and you probably bat a bit better. You can bat at number six or seven and be the second or third bowler.'

It made Greg feel great. 'Thank God I have a friend in the team.' He was going to need a few as some of the first class players did not immediately take to Greg's style.

His shield debut was against Western Australia at the Sydney Cricket Ground. Rick McCosker, the NSW captain, had never seen

Greg with Murray Bennett

Greg play. He asked Dirk Wellham what Greg was like as a bowler. Wellham gave his seal of approval and Greg was given the chance to bowl.

The West Australians took an immediate dislike to Matthews. They had heard that one of the attendants in the dressing room had called Greg 'Fred Matthews'. Greg was supposed to have said: 'The name is Greg Matthews. Remember it. I am going to be around for a long time.' Greg said he would never say anything like that. Once they spelt Greg's name with only one 't' on the scoreboard and he rang up and made them correct it.

The West Australians gave Greg a nickname, Colgate, for ring of confidence, and a hard time. They did not like the way he jumped in the air and carried on when he took the wicket of Geoff Marsh with his sixth ball but his scores of four and one restored their happiness.

After the game the veteran West Australian player, Tony Mann, came up to Greg and said: 'You better cool it if you want to last. You have to slow it down or the guys won't talk to you.'

Greg realised that Mann was trying to help and thought: 'Jeeesus . . . I am really going to be struggling in this game.' A few of his team-mates suggested he tone his act down. Again Murray Bennett provided support: 'Just be yourself. Don't worry.'

Michael Whitney the pace bowler from Randwick knows how Greg felt. He went through much the same sense of alienation when he started playing grade. He was picked for the State after a handful of games for Randwick. He was a Maroubra surfer with an earring. He only began playing cricket when he was 17 and when picked for the State seemed as though he had just traded in his surfboard for a cricket ball. 'It was very much the old school then of Dougie Walters, Trevor Chappell, Ian Davis and Peter Toohey, and they thought I was outrageous . . . I'm a lot like Greg in many ways . . . When Greg came along they did not exactly ignore him, but they did not go out of their way to talk to him. They thought he was crazy.'

The only people Greg got on with were Whitney and Bennett, who is a more straight-laced than the other two, but very tolerant. Whitney found Greg to be the only person he was really interested in becoming friends with off the field. Like the public he found it difficult to relate to the older style of cricketer.

Michael Whitney, Maroubra, 1980

If the old school could not see where cricket was going, Whitney could. Cricket really needed an injection of youthfulness and enthusiasm. He has made the whole public sit up and take notice and say, 'Who is this guy.' When he started taking a lot of wickets and making heaps of runs they were rapt. There are a lot of other good cricketers but they have not got the personality. Look at Craig McDermott, good fast bowler, nice guy and everything, but if you had to choose between him and Matho for a night out or a speaking engagement, you wouldn't even think about it.'

Greg develops a rapport with a wide range of people. Yet there are a few of the old school that he just cannot cop. He said of one Test player: 'He is a shocker of a human being. Absolutely no personality whatsoever. No get up and go. Does not put in when it does not suit him. An awesome talent, but an absolute shocker. I dislike it immensely if people don't try. It's not fair to his teammates.'

Bill O'Reilly was of an even older school and he immediately saw that Greg was different from the more recent school. Apart from noticing Greg for his bowling and enthusiasm, Bill O'Reilly was quite astounded at the way Greg would chatter incessantly on the field.

'He could not stop talking', O'Reilly said. 'He stood in the slips next to Rick McCosker and gave him a right old ear'oling, and I mean " 'oling," that's how you say it. Finally McCosker decided he needed some peace and quiet and he sent him to the covers. I don't think they like fielding too close to young Matthews. He tried to infect everyone with his bubbling enthusiasm.'

Greg recalls the conversation with McCosker a little differently. 'Rick would have told me to shut up if I had been saying anything that was detrimental to him, the team or myself. I was not making small talk, I was not asking him what he was doing in the evening or anything like that. I was talking about the opposition and the game all the time. It was my first game. I would ask what a player's name was, what did he do. Just cricket questions. Does he cut? Does he drive? Does he hook? Does he get out to slow bowling? All relevant stuff. And I would say this and that to relax me. Things to relax me.'

McCosker said of Greg a month later: 'It's great to have a young bloke in the team who thinks and talks about the game – he comes out with some pretty interesting things too . . . At the moment he just thinks it is a real buzz, that's his word, to play first class cricket.'

Greg was relegated to twelfth man for several games after his debut and was left out of the 12 for one match. During that first game Greg had been troubled by nerves. He spoke to Bob Simpson about the problem. Bob told him everyone got nervous. It was natural and useful to be nervous as the adrenalin flow sharpened the reflexes. The secret was to play the game ball by ball and accept the nerves.

Greg managed to fight his way back into the team for a game against Queensland in January. He scored an unbeaten 49 before NSW declared at five for 406. In Queensland's first innings he finished with the bowling figures of one for 17 off 13 overs. In the second innings he took three for 65 off 29 overs and helped steer NSW to outright victory. He was now certain to be picked for the next game at least.

After the match Greg said, 'The runs and the maidens helped my confidence and that is why I bowled better in the second innings. I just hope I can keep getting better and hold my place in the team . . . I have been with Gordon Nolan since I was eight and he is the most knowledgeable coach I have ever seen. He can pick up faults with his eyes closed and I owe him a lot.'

The following month Greg took the wicket of Greg Chappell and he had a headline to cherish: 'Greg falls to Greg.' He said: 'I was stoked after that. He was the man and I got him out. He liked to give young bowlers coming up a bit of a thrashing and put them in their place. I just got lucky and didn't receive the traditional thrashing. I was pretty happy to say the least.'

After five Shield matches Greg had scored 259 runs at an average of 51 and taken eleven wickets for just over 34 runs a piece. His performance helped NSW get to the final of the Sheffield Shield against Western Australia.

During the Australian winter of 1983 Greg took up an Esso Scholarship and played with another English club side, Worcester where he scored over 700 runs and took more than 50 wickets. He also played for the League Club side Old Hill scoring 1350 runs.

Greg thought the captain of Old Hill, Keith Wilkinson, was a great man. Greg loved his family, thought his kids were the best in the world and learnt much from Wilkinson about cricket. 'I still think back to the time I spent with him and the things he taught me.'

When Greg returned to Australia for the next season people started taking him seriously. In a one-day match against Queensland Greg set his field and a Channel 9 commentator said: 'He'll have to be a good bowler to bowl to that field.'

When Greg finished his ten overs with one for 29, Richie Benaud proclaimed, 'He must be a good bowler.'

Greg was bowling to an unusual field for a one-day game. He had a circle of men fielding reasonably close-in to the wicket to cut off any singles and only two men deep. His theory was pretty simple. He aimed the ball at the left-handers leg stump and had it spinning away. This made it very difficult for them to pierce the field. Benaud and fellow commentator Ian Chappell were so impressed they said Matthews could find himself in the Australian team that summer if he worked on his game a little more.

His big chance came when NSW played Pakistan at the SCG. While David Bowie was running through a few songs at The Sydney Sports Ground next door, Greg took four wickets and scored 86 runs. He had proved he could perform against an international team.

Bill O'Reilly began to publicly push for Greg's inclusion in the Australian team. He wrote in the *Sydney Morning Herald* the next day: 'At the moment Matthews is on the crest of an adventurous wave. In his latest innings he cut so loose on the Pakistani attack that no quick answer came to light and the young left hander excelled himself. When he finally faces a bowler who can fully test him, this young man will prove equal to the occasion.'

'His bowling is forceful, persistent and 100 per cent correct and reliable. He is a treasure to be envied by any captain on the lookout for a born fighter and a bundle of energy . . . Matthews who appeals to me as one who is unwilling to conceal any claims he has for instant recognition, is prepared to break into a gallop in his eagerness to settle down to business with the bat.'

Greg loved all this. He said at the time: 'I get a real charge out of people saying I'm in contention. It is good for me to hear people say that. It makes me go that little bit harder . . . I can't think of a better life than being a cricketer. This is what I've always dreamed of. Sometimes it still seems like a dream. I'll play for 15 years if I can keep my form and body together.'

On the strength of his performance in the State game against Pakistan, a solid Shield season, a shortage of all-rounders and the selectors desperate to find one, Greg was chosen for the Fourth Test against Pakistan at the Melbourne Cricket Ground beginning on Boxing day.

One cricket writer, Dick Tucker said Greg's rise reminded him of the Johnny Watkins story, which he described as the saddest in the past decade of test cricket: 'He was thrown to the wolves too soon and never recovered. The circumstances surrounding his sudden rise to Test status are almost identical to what could happen to Matthews.' To make matters tougher, Greg had only bowled on the Melbourne ground once and had described the pitch as terrifying, saying it was the flattest he had ever seen.

Gordon Nolan used to say: 'A boy should be a champion in his own division before he moves up to the next.'

THROWN TO THE WOLVES

The world was a different place for Greg Matthews, the Test cricketer, than it was for the Shield-playing version. The step from Shield to Test cricket is enormous. Hundreds of men get to play first grade, 66 get to play Shield cricket at any one time and only eleven get to play Test cricket. The gap in media coverage and public attention is even greater. Shield players strut their stuff before several hundred people and are occasionally seen on ABC television and described on ABC radio. Test players do their thing before 30 or 40 thousand people and have their every moment analysed by millions on commercial television.

And while the bulk of the planet don't care one way or the other about the outcome of a particular game in Melbourne, it was all terribly important to Greg. He had wanted to be a Test cricketer for as long as he could remember, had played his share of Tests against his brother Peter in the backyard, had copied the mannerisms of Test players as a teenager and now he was about to do the real thing. Nothing could be better than this.

Greg's family had supported him all through the years and were of course very proud. None more so than Neita. 'Just think, one of my boys is a Test cricketer. Only 12 people in Australia can be Test cricketers and, just think, an ordinary little fellow like my Greg is one of those 12. It is really something. We always knew he would play first grade, thought he might play for NSW and hoped he would play for Australia . . . Gordon Nolan had the most faith in him. He always said Greg would make it. It is such a tragedy that he was not here to see him in his first Test.'

Small parts of Greg's life had changed. Oaksie rode a motor bike

91

and Greg loved riding on the back of it. Greg had planned to get one. Oaksie was going to do the shopping for the bike. He looked at a few just as Greg's career was taking off. Greg was becoming more and more tied up with his cricket and somehow Oaksie never got round to putting the order in. Greg rang him one day and asked him if he had bought the bike. Oaksie said he hadn't. Greg said: 'Good, I can't take the risk of getting hurt . . . Mumma said so.'

All of a sudden journalists were interested in trivial pieces of information about Greg Matthews. At first it was fun, but after a while it became, as Greg said, 'A bit out of proportion'. By 1986 Greg would only give his phone number to selected people. However, Greg does make an effort to do the right thing. One of his favourite little sayings is: 'If you have your dance you have to pay the fiddler.'

So many people want fame and when they get it, they can't stand the hassle that comes with it. For a Test cricketer the tune is different and the price is much higher. Richard Hadlee, the great New Zealand all-rounder, found the pressure of being a cricket celebrity a bit much. 'I might be public property', he said 'but I enjoy my freedom and spare moments, and there are not too many of them. I've learnt to cope with the demands more by saying no to a lot of people. I just won't give that time any more.'

But it does not last forever and for some the fame is all too short. Just ask Michael Whitney, the NSW pace bowler. Nowhere has the rise from the relative obscurity of Shield cricket been more marked than with him. He was in England in 1981 playing cricket for a club called Fleetwood in the Lancashire League after a short stint in Sheffield Shield cricket. After several games Gloucester County gave him a trial, a big step up. During a Gloucester match, the manager of the Australian team, Fred Bennett, gave Whitney a call. As a result Whitney went from watching the West Indian pace bowler, Malcolm Marshall, bowl against Gloucester in the morning to a hotel room with Bennett and the Australian captain, Kim Hughes, discussing the next day's Test in the afternoon.

'We want you to bowl first change after Dennis Lillee and Terry Alderman,' Bennett said. That night Whitney roomed with Lillee, a long time hero of the 22-year-old's. The next day Australia lost the toss, England went into bat and Whitney was bowling in a Test match against England after only five Sheffield Shield matches.

'It changed my life,' Whitney said. 'I was a Test cricketer. It does not matter if you play one or 20 games, you will be a Test cricketer until you die. No one can take that away from you ... Mind you I would love to get some more scalps.'

It was a tough time to be playing for Australia. They had performed pretty well in the early Tests in England. They seemed to be set for a successful tour when they were involved in one of the more remarkable defeats in cricket history. Australia only needed to score 130 runs in the second innings of the Fourth Test to win. Ian Botham ran riot and England won. Once the wheel fell off the team on the field, other problems intensified. Hughes was captain but did not have the full support of the team. Marsh and Lillee had little respect for him and pulled in another direction. There was an undercurrent of antipathy between the players who had played World Series Cricket and those who had stayed with the Australian Cricket Board. To make matters worse, Rodney Hogg and Geoff Lawson were both injured, as was Carl Rackermann who was playing county cricket in England. Whitney was the only fit Australian pace bowler in England other than the two Test openers, Lillee and Terry Alderman.

There was not enough time for Whitney to become nervous for his debut. In the Fifth Test he took four wickets and felt happy with his performance and was selected for the Sixth. He was more nervous second time round and his figures were not as good. Since then he has been hampered by a bad back, knee and rib injuries and has not shown sufficient form to force his way back into the Test side. Greg's first big test started on 26 January, Boxing Day. On Christmas Day he went to the family home for a lunch of smoked salmon, king prawns and oysters. After an afternoon of drinking, talking about cricket, answering phone calls from well-wishers and reading cricket magazines, Greg went to Melbourne to join the team.

On Christmas evening Greg entered the Tapestry Lounge of the Melbourne Hilton where the Australian team were gathering before the Fourth Test. He wore a brown leather jacket, blue jeans and black calf-length suede boots and the earring. 'At least he left his motorbike outside,' one man in a blazer said.

On the day of the Test Greg was quite shocked by his state of mind. Greg is not always the most relaxing person to be around. Whenever he has to do something, whether it be filming a commercial, seeing Jillian, or getting to the ground on time, the feeling is one of absolute urgency. He always needs more sleep, desperately. He gives the impression that if he is not given every assistance with every little detail of his life the world will fall in around him. Greg has two speeds – asleep and hyper-active. Dave Gilbert said you just come to accept it when you know him well.

So on the morning of his first Test you would expect a bundle of nerves. But under real pressure he was calm.

Even though he found it awe-inspiring to share a dressing room with such cricket legends as Chappell, Marsh and Lillee, it made him positively excited rather than negatively nervous. Once he got into the dressing room he realised he was actually going to play with these guys. He drank in the moment.

As Neita said: 'Here he was with Greg Chappell and Dennis Lillee and Rod Marsh. He felt in awe of these great people and wondered how he could be part of a team with these greats. He was number ten or eleven down the line. They gave him a bit of hassle. Peer group pressure and all that. They were established Test players. Why would than want to talk to a young whippersnapper like G Matthews . . . Greg is not like that now [1986] when the young ones come in he makes sure he has the time to explain a few things to them.'

The heroes' halos did not stay in place long. Rod Marsh only ever said a dozen words to Greg and never gave him any advice or encouragement. Greg did not think Marsh's drinking exploits where anything to be proud of. But as he says, different strokes for different folks, 'It didn't bother me or phase me'.

When the team had a drink in the Hilton bar after that Fourth Test the established players were in a circle. Greg was half a seat back because he was not yet established.

Rod Marsh, Greg Chappell, Dennis Lillee, 1984

Marsh turned around to Greg and said, 'What do you think of when you play cricket for your country?'

'Well, if I can give it my best shot I am pretty happy.'

'That's shit. You have got three world record holders in the team and you should be out there trying to beat them.'

An example of the competitive nature of that environment had been demonstrated when Whitney was called into the Australian team in England. Whitney was very anxious to do well and felt a little unsure of himself because of the way he had been selected. In his opening spell he bowled a couple of bad deliveries and Marsh commented, 'Where did you learn to bowl? . . . Is that the best you can do?'

It is very hard to be a team player in a Test side. All the talk of doing it for your country can sound empty. The gap in salary and prestige between being in the Australian team and a Shield side is worlds apart. 'It [Test cricket] is different because it wears a different title,' Greg said. 'There is more pressure, more people watching, more expectations, more everything.'

Dirk Wellham finds Greg's attitude to the Australian team admirable. 'Greg really wants the Australian team on top, with the right kind of players in there. It is very hard to be a good team player when playing for your country because there is so much pressure to succeed.' The pressure is even greater in a losing side because the players know the selectors are looking for players to drop. In 1983 it was no longer a case of being harder to get out of the Australian team than into it.

When Bob Simpson was first in the Australian side the established players really did their best to help the new players out. That tradition faded after Ian Chappell became the Australian captain. The Ian Chappell approach was brash, confident and successful. After a game in 1972, Chappell, who had long sideburns at the time, said: 'I cracked myself when I got out. The ball came off the edge of my bat and flew up and hit me. It's sore now but I won't feel a thing tonight.'

Some commentators were impressed by Ian Chappell. Phil Wilkins said in the *Australian* that his leadership was strong and adventurous, he was a good spokesman for Australia and proved his qualities as a captain to those who doubted he was up to the job. It worked, but it was not cricket in the hooray-Henry sense. In 1975 Chappell wrote: 'You get a lot of people in the English game and even in the West Indies who say good morning to the fieldsman when going out to bat. That's a load of garbage as far as I am concerned. When someone says good morning to me I don't answer. I'm always willing to accommodate anyone who wants to have a chat on the field, but not a friendly chat.'

It was macho stuff and might have been the role model that influenced Greg as a youngster. Richard Hadlee, the great New Zealander said: 'When I first came into Test cricket to play against the Australians [1973-74] it was "kill, kill, kill, knock his effing head off" and that type of thing. It was all aggro, verbal abuse, the chipping away and calling you all sorts of names to upset your concentration. It was a technique, I suppose. A part of gamesmanship. It was probably an unfair tactic. That was the way I thought Australian cricket, Australian sport was played. That was their hard approach. It probably rubbed off on one or two New Zealanders in the end and probably hardened us up a little bit.'

The attitude had changed by the time Allan Border became Australian captain. During the First Test between Australia and New Zealand in 1985 Hadlee took 16 wickets, only three other bowlers had taken more than 15 wickets in a Test – Jim Laker, Syd Barnes and Bob Massie. 'At some stage every Australian player in Brisbane said, "Well bowled." That is something that never seemed to be heard from Australian players in the past. I enjoy the game so much more when it is played in such a way. That's what cricket is about; admiring performances even if it is the opposition. It is all a part of the scene.'

In 1983 the Marsh-Lillee-Chappell era was drawing to a close, but was not yet over.

Cricket politics were the last thing on Greg's mind just prior to the Test. He was far more nervous about his bowling than batting. He really did not have the experience to be a first string Test spin bowler. Bowling his first delivery was extremely testing. 'I was just freaking out.' He felt anything could happen. Greg mentally slowed himself down. He was bowling to Moshan Khan. His first ball turned out to be just a regulation delivery, reasonable length and the batsman came forward and played it down the wicket defensively. The crowd clapped. When he bowled his second ball it was a different sensation. By the time he finished the over he felt fine.

Being the only spinner put a lot of weights on Greg's shoulders. When Greg was fielding on the fence with the unspectacular figures of no wicket for 69, a spectator yelled out: 'You will never play for Australia again.'

Greg felt dreadful. He thought: 'I am playing for Australia and supposed to be a spinner . . . Jeesus'.

Greg was brought on to bowl again. His first wicket was Abdul Quadir, the talented spinner, who was on 48 and holding the Australians up. Then Azeem went for the slog and the ball flew to Geoff Lawson at deep mid-on who took the catch.

The second innings began well for Greg. He got the Pakistani opener Mudasser, LBW, in his first over and his spirits soared. He thought: 'Jeesus this is a good wicket to bowl on. Get 'em in there, line and length. Come on.' Zaheer Abbas, a great bowler of spin, was at the crease. Greg bowled round the wicket wide, the ball grabbed a bit of angle and turned a lot. It was one of the best deliveries he had ever bowled and it beat Zaheer. Greg's confidence went through the roof. 'Hang in there . . . hang in there' he thought. 'Come on.'

Dennis Lillee said that when he bowled his mental approach was to be pessimistic. 'Every time I thought, "I am going to bowl with a good rythm and pace and take five wickets." It almost never happened. When I thought it was not such a great wicket and I didn't feel so great, I got wickets . . . There is nothing worse than trying to predict success.'

Greg had Salim Malik on the ropes and was anything but pessimistic. Salim was prodding and missing a lot. Greg moved the slip at short leg. Salim lobbed one to that slip position. The field was changed back to what it had been originally and Salim lobbed a simple catch to the position where the fieldsman had been. 'It just was not my day,' Greg said. 'I was disappointed that I did not do a little bit better with the chance I had.'

It must be the most frustrating game in the world?

'It can be,' Greg said, 'but it is great for the character.'

There was one more character-building incident in the match for Greg. Fielding at point he dropped Abbas, who was on eleven off the bowling of Dennis Lillee. 'The papers said it cost us the test match,' Greg said. 'It certainly would have given us a better chance as he went on to score 55.'

At that stage of his career Greg's batting was far stronger than his bowling even though he had been picked as a bowler. Before going in to bat Greg felt unbelievably loose. He was not shaking, smoking 20 cigarettes or breathing heavily as he feared he might. He was chatting calmly to whoever was about. He felt good as he walked out into the crease and settled into his rhythm quickly. 'I remember Quadir threw one up high in the rough and I went down on one knee for a cover drive. It gave me great joy because I absolutely nailed it with a sweep. I thought Jeeesus what are you doing. You are not supposed to be doing that. You are supposed to be kicking them away. I remember feeling very jovial, smiling . . . And I was chatting away. Not deep in conversation but if someone made a statement, I would answer it politely and matter-of-factly?'

Greg got his 50. He was seeing the ball well, not playing and missing or scratching away for his runs. He was being patient and picking the ball to hit. He was doing everything right. 'I am going to be here for a long time,' he thought. 'Maybe I've got to hustle a bit more . . . Be positive . . . Think about it . . . Be aware.' After this private pep talk, his mind left the present and he began to think about scoring a century and how he could pay tribute to Mr Nolan. What a perfect way to pay tribute, that one minute silence.

'That was why I "odeed" at the umpire. I went over the top. It was a very spontaneous reaction. I hit it. I hit it and I looked up and he had his finger up.' The television replay showed that the ball went from the bat to the pad. Greg punched his bat and said: 'Oh . . . I hit it.' Greg turned and walked straight for the pavilion with large strides and taut body.

'I was thinking it was so unfair. There were 30 or 40 thousand people there. I did not stop to acknowledge them, which is rare because I normally always acknowledge the crowd if they applaud when I am walking to the pavilion. I just walked straight into the dressing room. No one said a word to me. The management came down. I was not reprimanded. I thought someone like Kim or Greg or Dennis would come down and really blitz me for doing that because it was obviously the wrong thing to do. Kim came down after about 20 minutes and said, 'Bad luck mate, did you hit it.'

Hughes did not allow journalists to interview Greg after the incident, but praised him for scoring an exceptional innings under enormous pressure. 'It was a remarkable hand for a guy who had played so little first class cricket,' he said.

Commentators outside the team were not so kind. The former English captain, Tony Greig, said Matthew's behaviour was disgraceful and he should be fined $500 for the incident which he described as a John McEnroe-type outburst. He did say though that Greg's innings was marvellous and was largely responsible for turning the Test around in Australia's favour. 'He has a tremendous future judging by his innings in a real pressure-cooker situation.' Greg and Graham Yallop's stand of 185 in 252 minutes was an Australian record for the seventh wicket in a match between Australia and Pakistan. Greg hit eleven boundaries. Yallop scored 268 and found Greg a different proposition from most cricketers: 'He is a very interesting character is our Greg. He's never short of a word. He suggested a few shots I should play. He is full of confidence. He probably will always be like that. He's a very useful all-rounder.'

Bill O'Reilly was impressed with the innings but unimpressed with Greg's reaction to his dismissal. He recalled the time Stan McCabe was given out LBW in a similar situation for 91 by umpire George Borwick. O'Reilly was next in to bat and walked past McCabe on the way out to the crease. Borwick asked O'Reilly what McCabe had said on the way to the pavilion. 'Not a word George,' O'Reilly replied, 'but a few spectators in the Members Stand told me they heard the tickle as clear as a bell.'

On the advice of Greg Chappell, Greg wrote a note to the umpire

Tony Crafter saying he was sorry for any embarrassment he might have caused. He also apologised to the team and the Australian Cricket Board official, Fred Bennett. It was a fine exercise in damage control. People seemed to be prepared to give Greg the benefit of the doubt, but he would not need to perform like that again. Greg learnt his lesson that day. You don't question an umpiring decision in a first class game, even if you are given out bowled after the wicket-keeper kicks the stumps over.

Dick French, a Test umpire who has controlled many matches in which Greg has played, is a fan of Greg the player and human being. 'He is very good with umpires, very respectful. He tends to call the umpire sir or umpire, which can be a bit off-putting when you are used to being called by your first name. I asked him why and he said, "I don't want to appear as though I am trying to suck up to the umpire in order to get favourable treatment." I think he has been unfairly blamed. People just don't understand him. I thought he learnt a lot after that dismissal in Melbourne. He is usually very good after a dismissal and I have seen him get some very doubtful ones. I think he is a very likeable young man. The New Zealanders think he is odd the way he sings and dances around ... The West Indians don't seem to care one way or the other what he does.'

French remembers umpiring a tense match between NSW and Queensland, Greg was bowling. Everyone was edgy. NSW had to win to reach the finals of the Sheffield Shield. Fieldsmen were clustered around the bat. French noticed that one NSW fieldsman had a foot on the wicket, which meant the next delivery would be a no ball. Greg bowled.

French called, 'No ball.'

Greg spun around and said, 'What was that for sir.'

'Peter Clifford has his foot on the pitch.'

'Oh beauty,' Greg said. 'I get another ball.'

French is most impressed with Greg's attitude as a cricketer.

'When he is fielding he tries to gee his teammates along by telling them to come on, get on with it, or keep it up, etc. His concentration when batting is very good. He is highly motivated.' So far everything seemed to be cruising along for Greg. He had proved he could score runs and take wickets in a Test and a regular position in the Test team seemed to be there for the asking. But there was still that nagging fear that he was not yet up to the mark as an international bowler. As Gordon Nolan used to say, 'Let the child become a champion in his own division before he moves up to the next.'

Greg had moved from State to Test cricket primarily on the strength of his bowling, had not played a full season of Shield cricket and had never taken five wickets in a first class game. He was a valuable part of the State team when he got the call to play for his country but not yet a champion.

After the Test series against Pakistan, won by Australia, Australia was to play in a one-day series against Pakistan and the West Indies. Pakistan were a reasonable batting side but their attack was at best mediocre for an international team. The West Indies had two champion batsmen in Vivian Richards and Clive Lloyd. Most commentators, including Greg, considered Richards to be the finest in the world at one-day cricket. In full flight he is awesomely beautiful to watch. Greg says if Allan Border had Richards natural talents his Test average would be well into three figures.

In early January, Greg was picked in the Australian team for the first one-day international match against the West Indies. 'One day cricket is different,' Greg said, 'how you go depends very much on who you bowl to and when. If you bowl to Viv or Clive at their peak when the match is well in progress, you are going to get a lot more runs hit off you than if you bowl to someone like Geoff Boycott in the third over.'

As fate would have it when Greg bowled his first over in an international one-day game, Lloyd had not been at the wicket long and Richards was about 30. Greg was hit for nine in that first over and thought: 'Oh no. I am going to get killed.' If they kept that pace up and Greg bowled ten overs his figures would be none for 90. Jeeesus. In his next over the West Indians only got one and it looked as though he might just hang in there. His spirits picked up. A few overs later Lloyd was dropped off Greg's bowling and then Larry Gomez came in and got two inside edges that went for four. Greg had 65 runs hit off him. 'It was a bad time to bowl,' he said.

Greg was not the only person to come to this conclusion. The *Sun*

103

wrote: 'Matthews was forced to bowl with Richards and Lloyd – the world's most dangerous batsmen – in full flight. While 65 is a lot of runs to score, it is difficult to imagine many spinners doing better against these two when they are well set.'

The nice thing about being an all-rounder is that you get another go. There were a few injuries in the Australian team and Greg was moved up the batting order to number five. This meant he would face the fastest West Indian bowlers when they were relatively fresh. He came in when Australia was three for 10.

'I was given out, caught off my hip. I was very disappointed as it was a slow pitch, it was a great opportunity. If I had scored 20 or 30 I might have been given the benefit of the doubt when my batting was having a few problems later in the season. I was primarily there as a bowler and did not come across.'

At least he won a few brownie points for the way he accepted his dismissal. The *Sun* wrote: 'Matthews scored only three before he was given out, from a delivery which appeared to come off his hip. It must have been terribly frustrating for Matthews, but he handled himself extremely well proving that he has benefited from the previous unfortunate incident.'

He had a chance to redeem himself against Pakistan. When he came on to bowl Javed Miandad was on 40 and Imran Kahn was on ten. They started forcing the pace almost as soon as Greg came on to bowl because they required almost six runs an over to win.

Greg conceded 51 runs in his ten overs, took two wickets, but was dropped for the next one-day game against Pakistan.

'I got my chance and blew it,' he said after he was omitted. 'But I have tasted what it is like at that level and I will be back. If every bowler conceded 65 and 61 in his ten-over spell, as I did, then we would be in a lot of trouble. Now I'm out to get five wickets and a ton for NSW against Tasmania on Friday.'

Greg was lucky he had Sheffield Shield cricket to go back to. It is a good safety net. If you get dropped at least it is not to complete oblivion. You are still a professional cricketer with a good team to play for. 'I love playing for NSW,' Greg said. 'It is the best domestic competition in the world. The Shield final in 1985 showed you can't get many better games. Fantastic game of cricket. It is a pity the public don't get into it a bit more . . . Team unity is fantastic. The best I have known. The guys get on. No individualism, it's a full-on team effort. It's good fun being part of the best. Good cricketers and good human beings, the boys who wear the blue cap.'

The match against Tasmania would prove whether Greg's confidence and ego had been seriously damaged by his one-day failures. Against Tasmania he had the chance to show the selectors what he was like in the face of a challenge. He came into bat with the score at four for 54. Greg and Peter Clifford had a fifth wicket stand of 149 in 171 minutes. The partnership was broken when Clifford attempted a lofted on-drive off the bowling of Mark Ray. He scored 74 in what was his Shield debut. Greg scored 72 off 142 deliveries and hit eight fours. He was out trying to loft Ray out of the ground. Greg Campbell began his match report in the *Australian:* 'Greg Matthews showed the fighting qualities required by Australia in its tour to the West Indies when he helped save NSW from a precarious position against Tasmania at Devonport Oval.'

Greg was selected for the 1984 tour of the West Indies. But it was never going to be easy. He loved the people there, got on well with the journalists, but struggled with his teammates socially and played very little cricket. Greg's brother, Peter, said that if Greg did not feel part of a team it affected his performance.

'I felt they did not like me as a human being,' Greg said. 'Towards the end of the tour more of the team came up and talked to me. I did not feel part of the side . . . It was a shocker . . . I did not play, very disappointed. I thought I had paid my dues and done pretty well in my first two Tests. I was given a token Test at the end of the tour'

'Touring,' Greg said, 'is different from playing at home. The captain, vice-captain and the third selector pick the team. You have social and playing responsibilities . . . If you are not considered a good guy to go out with . . . I spent a lot of time with the press guys.'

It did not help Greg's cause. As Phil Wilkins wrote in the *Australian*, 'One sometimes sensed that factors other than cricket skills might have been involved [in Greg's omission]; the cut of his hair, the distinctive tilt of his hat, his independent ways.'

The only way Greg was going to get into the Test team was if he could prove himself a better spinner than Tom Hogan. In an early tour match against Guyana Greg took only one wicket and Hogan took seven. After that Greg was on the outer and with John Maguire, Roger Woolley and the injured Carl Rackermann, he found himself as one of the test reserves and got very little playing time. He finally got a chance quite late in the tour against Barbados, who had won the Shell Shield. Greg bowled 31 overs in succession and finished with three for 83.

But still he did not look like forcing his way into the Test side. Then an opening appeared. Australia had been struggling to find an opener. Keppler Wessels and Graeme Wood were injured and had returned to Australia and Wayne Phillips was not delivering in that role. Hughes asked Greg if he would like to open the innings against the Windward Islands.

'Yeah! sure,' Greg said.

It was either opening the innings or batting number nine and his only chance of gaining Test selection. The pitch was good, Winston Davis opened the bowling and for once on the tour things went Greg's way. He and fellow New South Welshman, Steve Smith, put on an opening stand of 122.

Greg was selected for the Fifth Test played in Jamaica where he would face Joel Garner, Malcolm Marshall and Michael Holding. Greg only scored seven runs but he did hang around for a while and remembers that when Garner had bowled to the opening batsmen, his follow through took him half-way down the wicket. When Allan Border came into bat, his follow through took him to within two metres of the batsman. 'He lifted his pace by about three yards for Border,' Greg said. The West Indians target a team's best players. They gave England's David Gower the same compliment when England was there in 1986.

Does Greg hope that one day the West Indian speed demons will lift their pace for him?

'Yeah. It would mean I was doing something right, that they thought of me as a danger.'

Maybe one day, but when they bowled at regular pace in Jamaica Greg scored seven in each innings. Even though the scores did not excite anyone, people were impressed by his willingness to step into the breach and help out. He was only given two overs to bowl.

While the playing side of the tour was a disappointment, there were compensations. Greg loved going out in the West Indies. He loves to dance. 'In the West Indies,' he said, 'eighty per cent of the people danced 80 per cent of the time. The music was disco, reggae, steel bands and local stuff . . . Barbados had the most opportunities, there were heaps of discoes and nightclubs, more people, more options. It was the most westernised of the islands. Antigua was pretty quiet. There was one casino I spent quite a bit of time at. They had a few bands on there. In Guyana I went to the one disco all the time, it was a real dive. I went out with the press guys a lot.'

He enjoyed watching the games in the West Indies and not just for the cricket. 'The West Indians were fantastic. I struck up a really good rapport with them. There was this guy Forbes Burnham, who was the main man in Guyana, he came to the last day's play there . . . I got on exceptionally well with the people in the southern stand which is about 12 tiers deep, has wooden slab seats and piles of garbage on the dirt floor everywhere. Just general grottiness . . . They named the stand after me for the last half of the last day. I sat with this one guy I got on extremely well with. We would carry on, I can't say I had a few swigs of rum, but I can say we had a few drinks . . . Phil Wilkins wrote in the *Australian:* 'He was the darling of the West Indian crowd everywhere, always willing to talk, to sing and to throw a reggae hip.'

And as always there were a few lessons to be learnt. 'I learnt that the West Indies are the best team in the world and are the best to play against at the moment. Playing against the West Indies is probably the ultimate buzz in Test cricket. It was my first tour. You learn a lot particularly when you think back on instances that have happened . . . Hopefully I have learnt how to relate to the players and fit in with the first class scene better . . . People thought I was too much of an individualist and misconstrued my ideas of trying to help people and gee them up. I will try and tone that down. I had a talk to Dirk Wellham and he said there were no problem in the State team.'

On the tour Australia played 15 games, won two, lost six and drew seven. They lost the one-day matches three to one and the Test series three to none. In a report on the touring party in the Melbourne *Age*, Peter McFarline wrote of Greg: 'A rather different character to the normal sportsman, he nevertheless did all that was asked with enthusiasm and flair. Perhaps he did not get enough opportunities to improve his off-spin bowling. He could have been given a chance to partner Hogan before he finally made the Test team. At the moment, he is a batsman-bowler and it could be some time before he matures to the point where his slow bowling alone is justification to keep him in the Australian side.'

The selectors agreed and Greg missed out on the 1984 tour to India and was not in the 16-man squad given a contract by the Australian Cricket Board. Greg accepted his omission as being warranted after an uninspiring tour and was delighted that Murray Bennett had made it. One of his fantasies is that he and Bennett will one day be spin-twins for Australia.

After the Indian tour the Australians returned home to face the West Indies. It was a horribly difficult time for Australia to try and rebuild a Test team. Australia had to face the West Indies for ten tests in a row. No team in the history of the game had had a pace attack like the West Indians. Australia and every other team in the world were not even vaguely in the same class. The West Indies pace attack was frightening. The fastest was Malcolm Marshall, whom Greg regarded as the best in the world. When he tired there was no let up as Michael Holding and Joel Garner, the 6'7" human skyscraper, were on hand to continue the onslaught. They were not quite as fast but just as lethal.

Greg holds these men in high regard. After a match between NSW and the West Indies he told Holding that one of his dreams was to bat against him when he was bowling at top pace.

'Your bowling is so beautiful off a long run,' Greg said.

Holding, widely regarded as one of the nicest cricketing people in the world to run into off the field, said: 'You'll have to get into the Test team first.'

Easier said than done, even in these depressing days for Australian cricket. Greg had been performing consistently in Shield cricket, scoring 430 runs at an average of 35 a game, but had been overlooked for the first three Tests. Australia was outclassed and places were up for grabs by the Fourth Test. When NSW played Queensland, who were leading the Shield competition, Greg had a chance to push his claims. Greg scored 97 and took four for 81. He was selected for the Fourth Test and said, 'Hey man I'm stoked.'

It is one thing to be picked, it is another to perform. Greg batted at number six which he felt was too high for him. In one innings he let a ball go from the spin bowler and beautiful fieldsman, Roger Harper, and was bowled for two. Greg felt that performance was a disgrace. In the other innings he lasted an hour against Malcolm Marshall, who, with only one over to bowl before he was due to be rested, got Greg for five. Greg thought if he had just been able to hang in there a bit longer he might have been able to build an innings.

Greg was dropped. 'People expected things from me. I did not deliver ... It is never nice to get dropped ... That sick feeling.' However he never really felt his Test career was over, even though others said as much. After his success against Pakistan Greg knew he had the ability to score runs and take wickets in a Test match. He knew he had Shield cricket to go back to and he could build his game again there.

But Greg was not yet out of the news. After he was dropped from the Australian team, he had some time to kill in Melbourne. He and a friend went to the beach for a few hours and then went to the MCG to check on how the Australian team was getting on. Greg happened to be wearing a Hitler European Tour T-shirt and a photographer took a picture. It ended up in the papers. There were letters of protest. 'The T-shirt is both distasteful and distressing,' one *Sydney Morning Herald* reader wrote. 'I hope he [Greg] is never chosen again to represent his country.' Greg said the T-shirt was supposed to be a joke against Hitler. The cancellation of the British and Russian tour dates sent up Hitler's failure to occupy these countries, but as Greg points out, 'the pictures in the papers chopped that part out'.

To this point in Greg's life cricket was everything. But after he came back from the West Indies he would meet someone whom he valued above any game and who would give him the support and re-assurance he probably then needed.

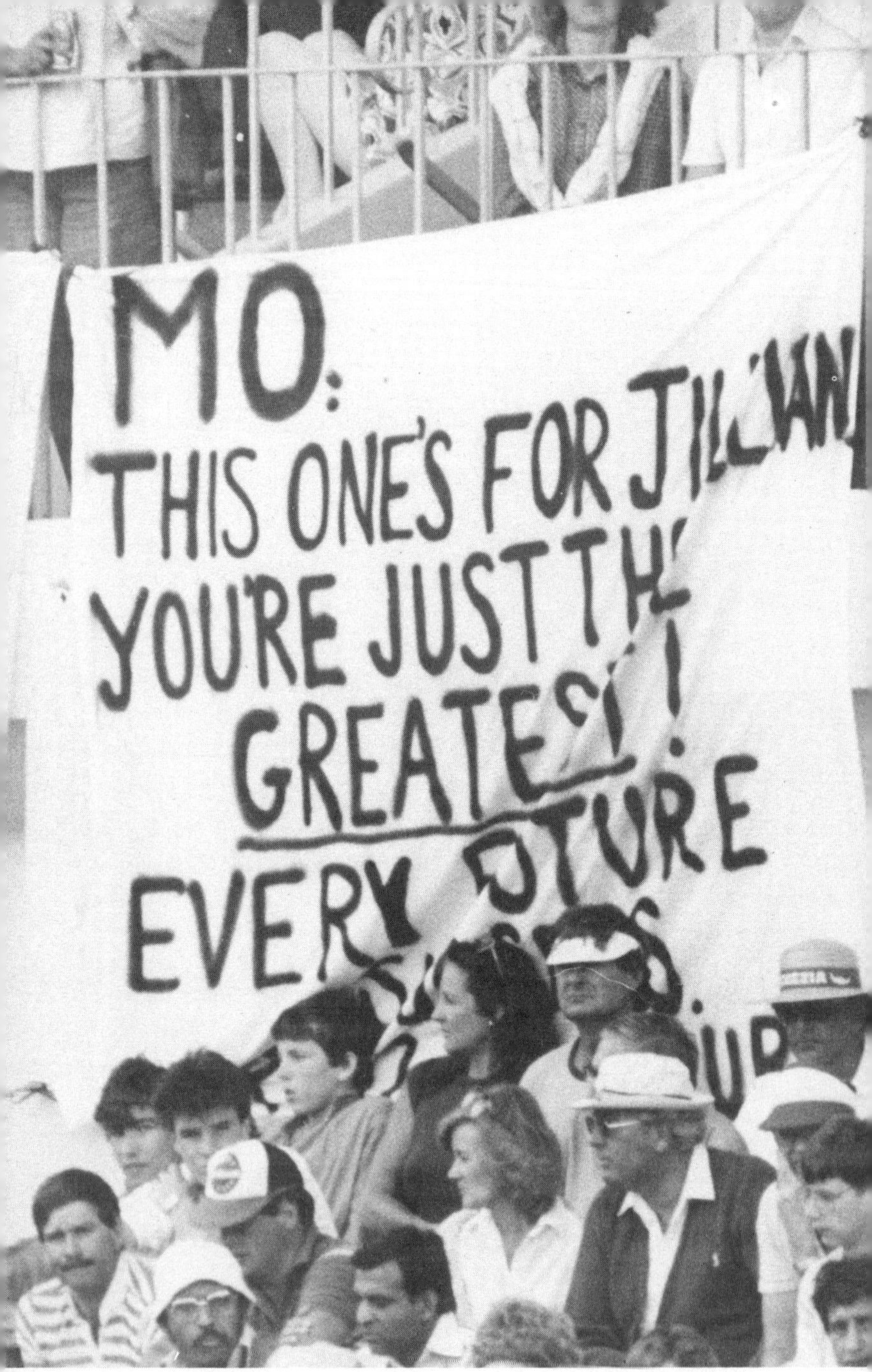
MO:
THIS ONE'S FOR
YOU'RE JUST
EVERY

JILLIAN

In early 1985 Jillian Clarke and her business partner, Julie Lenehan had been working hard for months at their fabric printing factory in Marrickville. They had been slaving late into the night most evenings and had not been out together for ages. When Julie suggested a night on the town, Jillian jumped at the idea.

A friend, Liz, had invited them out several times recently but they had always declined because they had been so busy. So they rang Liz to tell her they were going out the following Tuesday night and asked if she would like to join them. Liz had some good and bad news. The bad news was that she was going to a cricket dinner which sounded a touch dull. The good news was that the Pakistan all-rounder, Imran Khan, whose religion decreed that he was not supposed to have sex before he was married, was going to be there.

'Imran Khan', Julie said, 'We'll come.'

Liz said that if they arrived at 6 pm they would have to pay $15 to get in, but if they arrived at 8 pm they could be snuck in for nothing. They decided to get there at eight.

Before entering the rag trade Jillian had been to teachers college, but soon decided that was not for her. The next career path she explored was music, studying at the Conservatorium of Music in Sydney. She decided against that too and went to art school. Julie, her business partner to be, and childhood friend, was there. When Jillian left art school she worked in the art department of a fabric printing firm for three years. She then worked as a freelance fabric designer. Julie went overseas. Jillian took her job. When Julie came back to Australia three-and-a-half years ago, they decided to set up business together.

111

They started in the lounge room of a flat where they hand-printed material for the fashion designer, Jenny Kee, whom they have worked for ever since. The first shop they worked in was tiny. It had no electricity so the two could only work until sundown. When business picked up they knocked a wall out, then when business grew again they knocked out another wall. By 1985 they had built the business up to such an extent that they employed eight people. The following year they decided it made more sense to employ only one extra and work longer hours themselves. So the night out on Tuesday was something to look forward to.

The cricketers club sounded pretty swish – famous cricketers, cocktail waitresses and glamorous women in long dresses. The fact of the club fell far short of their fantasies. As Greg said, 'It's not Jillian's territory at all.'

On the big night Julie and Jillian took steps to ensure they were not outshone. They decide to wear backless dresses, have their hair elaborately done and their faces carefully made up.

They arrive at the club and are snuck in for free. They walk into the main ballroom to check the scene. It is not what they had imagined. 'It was really straight' Jillian said later. So they get a drink and walk around the balcony wondering how to amuse themselves. At first glance the scene looked impenetrable and they were not sure if it was worth penetrating.

Meanwhile Greg is talking to a friend of Jillian's.

Jillian spots him. 'Who's he?' she asks Julie. Julie does not know. Jillian continues: 'He's cute . . . Liz did we go to school with him or something.'

A girl nearby overhears the conversation and says: 'He's Greg Matthews.'

'Who's he?' Jillian asks.

'He used to play cricket for Australia.'

'How does he play?'

'Not very good.'

Jillian was feeling on top of the world. 'I don't want to know him. Give me a star. I want a star.'

She got what she wanted in the long run. 'Now he is a star,' she

112

Greg on the night he met Jillian

said. 'It is my positive thinking. I knew that he would do well. He is just that type of person. He would do well in anything he put his hand to.'

Back to the cricketers club. Greg has a pint of Old beer in his hand and his suit on. He is chatting away in his normal animated fashion. He turns his head and sees Jillian. He turns his head away, reflects on what he has seen and turns his head dramatically back to gawk at Jillian.

Greg is not the sort of guy who will sit in a corner and suffer from social dread when he spots someone he fancies. His confidence is not restricted to the cricket field. He is not one who thinks it inappropriate to make a move and say hello. Greg likes to be on the front foot in the social context. He thinks nothing of bowling up to someone and initiating a conversation. He walks over to where Jillian and Julie are talking. A mutual friend says: 'These are two friends of mine.'

Greg is never lost for words and is a bit of a ladies man. He always knows what to say. No mundane comments from Greg. 'I really like your hair', he tells Jillian.

Jillian smiles and says: 'Thanks.'

Greg kept things flowing with, 'How old are you?' Which was not the ideal comment as Jillian is older than Greg and after all the chap is supposed to be older than his sweetheart.

But things went fantastically well. The pair just clicked. It was love at first gawk. The bells were ringing. They had a few beers, many laughs, left the club and went and sat by the harbour and talked for hours. Jillian drove Greg back to his car and they talked for another hour.

'I was in really good form that night,' Jillian said with a click of her fingers. 'Right in there with those quick one liners, we had a fantastic night. I never felt so natural with a person . . . We just beat the garbos home.'

Neita Matthews said it was on the second night that they really got to know each other. When I mentioned this to Greg he laughed, 'We had an outrageous night . . . A lot of laughs.'

Greg asked Jillian to go out with him to a NSW team dinner on the following Friday night, the eve of the final of the State one-day competition known as the McDonald's Cup. Jillian had to go to dressage training, but was still keen to go out. Greg asked her to meet him after that at the restaurant where the team was eating.

After the dinner they went to a pub in Balmain where they listened to jazz. They took up where they had left off at the cricketers club. 'We had a funny night," Jillian said. "Great night. We laugh a lot. He is really funny, a scream . . . He is really nice. Really to the point.'

There is no censoring mechanism in Greg's brain to filter out information from the brain before it reaches the mouth.

'I know, I know,' Jillian said.

Jillian dragged a friend along to see Greg play for NSW in the final of the McDonald's Cup. At this early point in their relationship Jillian could not have understood the pressure Greg was under on the field. Because the critics had written Greg off as Test match material after the West Indies series, he desperately needed to get amongst the runs to have any chance of being selected for the Ashes tour of England at the end of the season.

There were not too many games left. He needed to start scoring runs sooner rather than later. Unfortunately his omission from the Fifth Test team had had a domino effect. Originally he and the NSW selectors thought he had been selected for the Fourth and Fifth Tests, so he was omitted from the NSW team for the McDonald's cup semi-final against Victoria. He sat in the grandstand while NSW won by seven wickets.

In the first Shield game against Victoria he scratched for an hour-and-a-half to score 13 runs. He bowled well but ended with the unflattering figures of one for 91. The next game against Tasmania was not much better. He was out for five runs and then bowled only eight overs in the first innings. Nothing seemed to be sliding into place.

Greg has never really had a horror stretch, but he has had his share of rough trots, and the post-West Indies period was threatening to become a shocker. Cricket can be the most frustrating exercise on the planet. The line between hitting the ball in the centre of the bat and catching an edge is only a few frustrating centimetres wide.

During a horror stretch getting the damn thing to hit the centre of the bat consistently seems impossible.

'When I have disappointing runs I don't seem to have the confidence in myself to move my feet and strike the ball', Greg said. 'Don't seem well co-ordinated. You don't hit the ball as sweetly. The timing goes off. You can't put the ball where you want it. When you are bowling you tense up. You don't relax as much. Being relaxed gives you a better opportunity to make the ball spin. It has never happened to me fielding. I have never fielded when I thought I would let myself down or disgrace myself. It's my tower of strength. I love it. You just go out there and give it your best shot.'

Sometimes things go wrong during a match. 'You get a bit tired mentally and physically. The batsmen might gain a bit of a psychological edge. They get an advantage . . . You should never give in but you wonder what to do, where to bowl. You feel there are no answers. You say in your mind all the things you were taught, but you can't get it together at the time. Control of the head . . . people do it better. Go back to the basics of course, short stride . . . Most important to slow things down. Take your time. Dirk Wellham is quite good like that. He comes up to you if you have been hit for a couple of boundaries and gives you time to think.'

Wellham often talks to Greg about his cricket in a social context, particularly when things go badly. He also gives practical help when possible. In the second innings of the match against Tasmania there was nothing hanging on the last day's play and Wellham gave Greg 20 or 30 overs to get his confidence back. He took two for 86 and thought he deserved better.

Who knows what get's a player out of a slump. In Greg's case it would be nice to think it was Jillian, with a touch of Wellham, that did the trick. Whatever, something went right in that McDonald's Cup final. As Phil Wilkins wrote in the *Australian:* 'The setbacks rocked Matthews . . . But Greg Matthews, 25, is a vibrant cricketer whose steely resolve and shrewd cricketing mind are well cloaked by a facade of free spirit. While the ego was not harmed, his pride in performance was certainly frayed at the edges. The McDonald's Cup final win over South Australia proved the turning point in the

116

summer for after making runs he fielded and bowled superbly to take three for 29 in the Cup win.'

Greg was on a roll. In the Shield game against Queensland he was man of the match. 'I was lucky', Greg said. In the first innings he took three for 22 from 16.5 overs and five for 32 from 22 overs in the second innings. To top it off he scored 87 runs in five hours to help NSW win by 61 runs.

The roll continued when NSW played Victoria in the next Shield game. Greg came in when the score was four for 91 and scored 103 to post his maiden first-class century. When his score moved into three figures, he ran over to where his mother was sitting and paid tribute to her for the part she had played in his success. 'Mumma always comes and watches me play,' he said. 'She knows all about pressure. It was very important for her because she gets into it. She's a very knowledgeable lady.'

At the crease with Greg was Stephen Waugh. During the tour of the West Indies the year before Greg was singing the praises of Waugh whom he said would score 4,000 runs in Test cricket and be a true champion. The other players laughed at Greg and rubbished him for making such outlandish suggestions. In 1986 the same men came up to Greg and said, 'You were wrong, he is better than that.'

When Greg is impressed he does not beat around the bush. Waugh is no exception. 'He is greatness', Greg said, 'he has more ability in his little finger than I have in my whole body.' Yet Greg did not do badly that season. He had aimed to score over 600 runs and take 20 wickets in Shield cricket. He scored 684 runs, took more than 20 wickets and turned in some match winning performances. ''For an all-rounder,' Greg said, 'that is pretty good.'

Jillian certainly did not hurt his cause. Greg's batting seems to be helped when there is someone in the crowd with whom he is especially close. 'It may sound stupid, but if there is someone there I feel particularly close to it helps. I feel good vibrations or something. If there is someone there it makes a difference.'

While Jillian gives Greg great support and is right into the cricket side of his life, she is very much her own woman doing her own thing and does not live her life vicariously through Greg. She works

118

extraordinarily hard. She sets the alarm for 6 am so she can be at work by 6.30. Greg struggles to be on deck by 10 am. Jillian often works until 8 pm and rarely takes time out for lunch. When business is busy she is quite happy to work on Saturdays.

I heard someone ask Greg, 'Why doesn't Jillian sit back and take it easy?'

'She has her own thing to do', Greg said.

The support goes both ways. 'He gives fantastic support', Jillian says, 'he scrubs pots and drops things off.' When I was interviewing him one day he said he would rather be with Jillian slopping paint than sitting with me discussing him. 'He's mad', Jillian said, 'it's freezing cold, our factory used to be a storage place. But he likes being there watching me work. He's crazy.'

Jillian enjoys watching Greg at work. 'I think I help him', she said. 'I feel just as positive about him as he feels about me. He has always been more positive about my career and I have always been more positive about his. We have these discussions about how positive we are and stuff.'

Greg says that behind every great man is a greater woman. He thinks highly of himself and judging by the amount of time and emotional energy he devotes to Jillian, she is way up there. She has a special influence on Greg. Nowhere is the strength of their relationship more tested than in the car. Greg is an Olympic Class backseat driver.

Greg used to drive Oaksie mad. 'Why don't you change lanes, that will be quicker . . . accelerate you can take him . . .?'

'Shut up Greg, who's driving?'

Greg would laugh the complaint off and say something like: 'Don't be a dickhead Oaksie we are running late. If you got caught by those lights we would have been stuck there for five minutes.' Oaksie would keep driving and Greg would keep on advising.

With Jillian it was another story, says Oaksie. One day the three of them were in the car. Jillian was driving. Greg said, 'Let's turn right up here.'

'Shut up Greg I am driving,' Jillian said.

A little later Greg said: 'Why don't you overtake him?'

Jillian hit the brakes, pulled over to the curb, got out and said 'Greg if you are not going to shut up. You drive.' Greg took over the wheel and was subdued for the rest of the trip. 'He just did not know what to do,' Oaksie said, 'If it had been me pulling a stunt like that he would have said: "Come on Oaksie don't be a dag." '

Greg recognises the Jillian factor. 'I used to party a lot. I used to lead a super-active social life. When I was 24 or 25 I just seemed to change. Don't know why, I guess I have had other things to do. More music .. go to more people's places. Things just slowed down. Maybe I just found what I wanted. I don't know.'

His mother has a fair idea. 'Greg is much more settled now. He and Jillian get on very well. They blend together. She has her own ideas and is a successful businesswoman. The relationship is more stable with them both doing well . . . When you are playing the field you have different friends. All sorts of hours. When you are settled you don't want to go out raging. You don't want to do all that.'

Jillian says Greg still knows how to party, perhaps there is just less of it. They spend a great deal of time watching tele, eating and talking.

But Greg is wrapt in his new lifestyle. 'We just get on so well. I relax around her better than anyone else.' And its good for his cricket. 'It's good to hear good positive talk. It's good for my game it lifts a lot of pressures. Like Mr Nolan it gives me a certain amount of confidence. She enjoys watching and I enjoy having her there.'

The worst thing for Greg about being picked on the Ashes tour in 1985 was that he had to be away from Jillian. It would have been a good investment if he had taken her with him. But when he was selected he was delighted. 'Oh goody – good one.'

On the tour Greg seemed to get on with the other players much better than he had in the West Indies. It was partly because Greg knew them better and they knew him, and partly because some Australian players had accepted a fortune to play in South Africa rather than represent their country and this seemed to bring the Australian team closer together.

Some of the English journalists were not quite so sure what this Greg Matthews character was all about. Frank Keating, the columnist

Above: Jillian, Greg and Neita

Below: At home

from the *Guardian*, described Greg in his book about Ian Botham, *High Wide and Handsome*. 'I think the counties anyway will take to Greg Matthews, the off-spinning bits and pieces man. His every ball is a fizzing wicket taker judging by the oohs and ahs after every delivery. You know the type – every village opposition side has one. You can dispatch him for miles, or at least to the next field: Phew he grimaces and tells you in sign language how lucky you were to lay a bat on the thing. The young man has not yet learned to bowl more than five good balls an over – but when he does he could be very, very useful, especially if his batting comes on in tandem. In craggy response, his profile looks not unlike a gritty young Doug Walters: when the sixes fly over the hedge and the defiant oohs and aahs, he goes back to his mark simpering and sad as Stan Laurel. Matthews is built like a junior light-welterweight, and he has had his Sydney barber crown him with a jutting-prowed, punky-proud crew-cut. When he was introduced to the press at Heathrow, one sage reckoned he looked as though he was about to be deported to the colonies rather than having just transported himself from them.'

It reminded Keating of when Henry Blofeld, who came from the social heights of Eton, entered Australia and had to fill in a form. The first question was: 'Have you a criminal record.' Blofeld looked at the customs official and said, 'My dear old thing, I didn't realise it was still obligatory.'

On the field things began well for Greg. He was selected for the one-day series. Australia lost two quick wickets, including that of the team captain, Allan Border, who thought Australia would be struggling. But Greg, Wayne Phillips and Geoff Lawson did enough to win the match. Greg hit the winning runs and was not out 29. He bowled economically and took one wicket. 'No sweat man,' Greg said after the match, 'I had a job to do and went out and did it.' The journalist covering the match for the *Australian,* Terry Brindle, said: 'Matthews is either plain loco or genuinely eccentric, depending on your charity.'

The wicket he got was a beauty, that of Botham. England had batted first and had lost Fowler, Gower and Lamb. The score was three for 27 when Botham came in. Graham Gooch and Botham had added 116 in 28 overs. Bob Holland took Gooch's wicket. Botham then twice hit Holland over the mid-wicket fence for six. Greg was brought on to bowl. Botham greeted him with a six. Shortly afterwards Botham hit Greg for his fifth six. Greg bravely tossed up another one. Botham waited, went down on one knee and attempted a reverse sweep. He missed and was bowled. Botham was out for 72 off 82 balls.

Like Greg, Botham draws an enormous amount of publicity. But unlike Greg his play can be more unorthodox than his personality. The general consensus among cricket followers was that the stroke was extraordinarily irresponsible. 'Botham Sweeps to Disaster' echoed the tabloids. The chairman of the English selectors, Peter May, said: 'I have thumbed through the MCC coaching manual and found that no such stroke exists.'

Botham was not too fussed. 'When all is said and done', he said, 'this was one of my tamer dismissals . . . Anyway in this game they forget to give the bowlers the credit as well. So, good for Greg Matthews, I'd charged him the previous ball and it had cleared mid wicket for six. So I expected a flatter delivery; 99 per cent of the spinners in the world would not have tossed up the next one. So jolly good luck to Greg, he is already a jolly good cricketer; this proved it didn't it? A bubbly personality, too. I think he's going to be really useful for Australia in the not-too-distant future. He's enthusiastic, a real individual, and his own man – he goes for it in his own way.'

Botham writes a column in a British newspaper and Greg read comments similar to the above in the paper. Greg was blown away. 'It was exactly how it happened. As I ran in I thought, toss it up, that's what I should do and I did. Don't know why just one of those things. I tried something and it came off. For a spinner, it is a fantastic feeling when something like that works.'

Botham predicted good things for Greg. 'Greg Matthews came to England and I said to a lot of people he will do well. They looked at me and said, "He is just a clown. He will not do anything." I said that does not matter. I said the guy wants to play. The guy lives and breathes cricket. He has a certain amount of natural ability, so combined with the will and determination he will come through.'

There is one off-field anecdote worth injecting. When Greg tried to get into a disco at Cambridge, the guard refused to let him in because he thought it would lower the tone of the place. 'We don't want the kind of publicity that a London nightclub got when they admitted Jeff Thompson with a dolly bird', the ever-watchful bouncer said.

Things did not go much better on the field. After his solid one-day efforts, Greg through he would be a chance for the First Test, but was not picked until the Fourth Test. In the first innings he did nothing with bat or ball. In the second innings, Keppler Wessels did not want to open. Allan Border asked Greg if he would like to. 'Sure', he said. 'I thought if I was in there I might be able to build something. I knew it was my last chance. If I did not play well I might not get another chance.' He scored 20-odd and did not play again on the tour.

Jillian never lost faith in Greg. She knows he is the kind of guy who can pull that bit extra out when it counts. 'He has always done phenomenal things', she said. "Did you see that run-out in the Fourth Test? It was amazing. Did you see how far away he was. He is always doing phenomenal things.' Greg had run Allan Lamb out for 67.

Jillian says Greg is an excellent tourist. 'He always sees what has to be seen and does not waste his time. He always buys things from those countries he visits . . . In the West Indies he bought a bottle of rum. He bought carpets from India. He buys jewellery, clothes, all sorts of things.'

At first Jillian was only interested in cricket when Greg was involved, but as she started to understand the game and got to know the players, she became more interested in the whole process. 'I hear them talking about the opponents so you get a feeling of what they are like too and that makes it even more interesting.'

When Greg returned to Australia he was anxious to re-establish himself. He did just that against Tasmania. Jillian was flying down to see Greg play on the Saturday morning. Greg went in to bat. Jillian boarded the plane. En route she tried to find out the score but with no success. She arrived at the airport. Greg moved on to 98. Jillian took a taxi to the ground. Greg hung in there. She arrived at the

ground. Greg was at the crease. His name on the scoreboard had 150 next to it.

'It was a free 200', he said. 'I should have got 200. I got a long hop from Mark Ray. I laid the ears back and really tried to power it, instead of easing it over the fence. I skied it and was caught [for 184]. It was a shortish boundary. I was really disappointed.'

In the next game Victoria had by far the better of the first three days play and needed only 169 to win on the last day. Celebrations with champagne and ticker tape were prepared for them in Melbourne.

Greg scored 35 and 28 with the bat, and was anxious to redeem himself with the ball. 'That's why I love being an all-rounder', he said. 'You get two chances.' Wellham was originally only going to bowl Greg for one over after lunch so could switch his bowlers.

Bob Simpson had a word to Greg as he walked onto the field after lunch. 'Take one', Simpson said, 'and then make it five.'

Greg is very coachable. In the first over he took the wicket of Simon O'Donnell, the man with whom he was vying for a spot in the Test side against New Zealand, was kept on and took another four wickets to finish with five for 22. Victoria were all out for 78. Greg went behind the scoreboard to console the Victorians.

A telegram was sent to Melbourne: VICTORIAN CRICKET ASSOCIATION STOP JOLIMONT STOP MELBOURNE STOP URGENT CANCEL TICKER TAPE STOP TAKE CHAMPAGNE OFF ICE STOP SIGNED RAY BRIGHT STOP

So Greg was picked for the First Test against New Zealand at the Gabba in Brisbane. For years Australia had always thought of New Zealand as poor neighbours who never quite deserved to be in the same ball park. However, in 1985, the Australian team were in no position to condescend to any one, let alone New Zealand who had developed a confident and professional team. They were one of the few teams to take a Test series from Clive Lloyd's West Indies team. They won a series in Pakistan and almost took a series from England in England.

They did not have an abundance of gifted players but they did have a solid outfit with several outstanding individuals. Jeremy Coney, with whom Greg never really managed to get any conversation together despite repeated efforts on Greg's part, was an astute and respected captain. And Martin Crowe, whose brother Geoff also played for New Zealand, is a batsman of 'enormous potential', said Greg, 'he moves well, has tons of natural ability . . .'

The most important man in the New Zealand team was Richard Hadlee, the great all-rounder. In the *Sydney Morning Herald,* Mike Coward wrote, 'It is principally because of Hadlee that New Zealand Cricket has come of age.' At 34 he was no longer an express bowler, but, like Lillee and Holding before, he was a master of seam and swing with the ability to subtly vary the pace, bounce and angle of his deliveries. Greg said even though Hadlee was not super quick he was still one of the world's most dangerous strike bowlers.

In many ways Jillian gets more nervous than Greg during a match. He is used to the pressure of only being as good as his last game. One day over a drink with Jillian the conversation turned to the coming season, Jillian's eyes flicked around the room and she said: 'I just hope he does well this season.'

Does Greg worry?

'No he loves it all.'

Jillian agrees they are both hyperactive creatures. Greg does not like to gossip or tell stories, which makes him a touch difficult to interview. I felt more comfortable with Jillian than Greg, who is often on an offensive defensive. 'What do you mean by that?' he will ask if he thinks you are saying something he has doubts about.

The only thing that Jillian does not like about Greg is that his cricket takes him away from her for large stretches.

'He has to travel for seven months of the year', she said. 'It's pretty glamorous. A lot of women out there.'

Jillian is friendly with all the women who watch their husbands and boyfriends play for Australia, but she likes to watch Greg play so that he can 'lock in on the vibes.'

Cricket celebrity does open a myriad of possibilities. But Greg and Jillian only have eyes for each another. 'Better to have quality than quantity,' Greg said. Time with Jillian is precious to Greg. She arrived during an interview session at Greg's house. Greg said quietly but firmly, 'Better split soon.'

127

They speak constantly on the phone when Greg is away cricketing. If one of them is late answering they say: 'Were you out with your OM (or OW).' OM and OW is their joke for another man and another woman.

The First Test against New Zealand was the first opportunity Jillian had had to watch Greg play in a Test. Jillian arrived in Brisbane on the Thursday. When she arrived at the ground the next day Australia were seven wickets down. 'Greg must not have batted', Jillian thought. He had been bowled for two.

To make up for the batting failure, Greg took three wickets. He had the opener Wright LBW with a ball Murray Bennet had taught him to bowl that skids on. Greg's next victim was Jeff Crowe, who had been batting aggressively. Greg held a delivery back. Crowe came down the wicket to belt it out of the ground and instead lobbed it into 'Pop' Holland's hands at deep mid-on. Greg's final wicket was a lucky but good one, Martin Crowe. At the end of his spell, Greg began to tire a little and Hadlee wacked him for 20 or 30 in a couple of overs and he was taken off.

The night before the Test was the most trying as both were anxious about the following day and the possibilities it held. By Remembrance Day the show was on the road and the uncertainty had eased. But by the time Greg was to bat the intensity returned. Jillian was at least as nervous as Greg.

A DAY TO REMEMBER

As usual Greg slept in on 11 November 1985. He loves bed and will forgo breakfast to spend extra time there. He is forever saying, 'I have got to get my sleep . . . I neeed my sleep.' He rarely sees the mornings on the weekends. When on tour, he nearly always sleeps for as long as possible, has a shower, grabs his kit, then goes downstairs to join his teammates to catch the bus to the ground. He figures he can always get a couple of sandwiches and a cup of tea when he gets there. Greg is more likely to have breakfast when he is overseas, particularly if he is staying in a hotel with a restaurant that impresses him.

Jillian is not as addicted to sleep or cricket as Greg. She is insufficiently fascinated by cricket to sit through a day's play without Greg being out there. On the day of the Brisbane Test she elects to stay at the hotel when the team goes off to the ground in their bus. She wants to take her time getting ready. Jillian enjoys staying in expensive hotels and likes to make the most of it. To her it is better value lying in the sun by the hotel pool than rushing to the ground to watch strangers at play. It is not a bad life this Test cricket.

It is not as much fun for the Australians out at the Gabba. The day before had been very tough. The New Zealanders had an almost unassailable lead. They had scored 553 for the loss of seven wickets in their first innings in reply to Australia's 179. The pressure was right on. The Australians had received a hammering on the field, from the television commentators and in the papers.

'The Australian dressing room,' Terry Brindle wrote in the *Australian*, 'was a tomb reached with drab regularity along the Rue Morgue . . . Australia's early batting was a doleful procession stricken with every sign of defeatism and riddled with the self-doubt of men entitled, if they were realistic enough, to question their ability at Test level.'

The New Zealanders were on a roll. It was a great time for them to be bowling. The day before Australia had been in the field forever. They were mentally and physically exhausted. The New Zealand bowlers felt great. After a night's sleep the Australian players were physically fresher, but still under great emotional and psychological pressure. They knew that if the team failed as miserably as seemed likely, the selectors would be sorely tempted to make wholesale changes. Under these circumstances everything seems to go wrong. 'They find the edges,' Greg said, 'and bang you are gone.'

When the going got excruciatingly tough for Sherlock Holmes he used to tell his mate, 'Just remember Watson the greater the adversity the greater the triumph.' Greg can relate the Holmes philosphy to cricket. Great innings are only great because they are made when it counts. The time it counts is when your side is on the rack and everyone around you is losing their heads and wickets. It is the time when most players would rather be at the beach, playing golf, having a beer, anywhere but at the batting crease. Greg likes to think this is prime time for him.

Well this was Greg's chance to see if his self-image matches the reality. As Greg sits waiting to bat, his teammates, with the exception of Allan Border, are puttings up token resistance. It seems as though none of them are up to the task. Ex-players, the public, commentators, journalists and anyone else with half an interest in the game shake their heads with disbelief. It is one thing to be thrashed by the West Indies, they give everyone a hiding, but New Zealand? Who would want to be part of this second-rate Australian team?

Greg is not phased. He relishes the opportunity to do something great for his country. He knows it is a good wicket and is playing true. New Zealand had proved it is not impossible to score runs on this pitch. They had made it all seem ridiculously easy.

In a way it is a good time for Greg to bat. His thoughts are positive. The Gabba had always been kind to him. Apart from a two in his first innings his lowest score there had been 49 not out. And even though it is traditionally much more of a seamer's than a spinner's wicket, he was always able to get one or two wickets here. While he wants his comrades to succeed more than anything, he enjoys the thought of going in and doing well when all others are falling about him. The prospect of the heroic challenge lifts rather than deflates him. 'I had a chance to do something really great for Australia that day,' Greg would say later.

At the family home in Ryde, Neita Matthews is sitting by the television. Only eleven men are good enough to represent their country in a Test match. Neita just can't believe one of her boys is one of those eleven. Whan an honour. Even if his position is a bit shaky, it is her boy and he can do anything; she knows as well as anyone; she has seen it often enough. All the same it seems amazing that an ordinary chap like her boy Greg will be out there soon with everyone watching.

Back at the Gabba, Greg feels very good. He is charged with expectant anxiety. He has confidence in his abilities. He has been groomed for this. It is his prime time. While his teammates are struggling on the pitch, Greg listens to the rock band Midnight Oil on his Walkman. The Oils give Greg an energy lift. He wriggles his shoulders to keep loose.

Greg does different things before he goes in to bat depending on the mood. Sometimes he has the Walkman on with the Oils blasting away, sometimes he chats to teammates and occasionally he will have a snooze. 'I try to sit back and visualise possible strokes and deliveries, trying to get positive thoughts into the mind,' he said. 'The key lies in conjuring positive images.'

Greg has extended or reduced the cliche, 'treat every day as though it were your last', to cricket. 'I try to have the attitude that every day I play cricket it will be my last day and I try to make it my best day. It is not perfect every day and it is all relative, but I like to give myself a chance of doing it . . . I try to get better. I don't know about excellence.'

As the Oils charged him up he said to himself, 'Be positive. The wicket is good. You can cut it. You have got to be positive. Be positive. Hustle. Be positive. Think about it.'

Back on the field, Ritchie was caught for 20 by Jeremy Coney off the bowling of Chatfield. It is Greg's turn to bat. He walks out to the crease. He reminds himself: 'Be positive . . . Hustle . . . Remember your responsibilities.' He feels good. Jillian is in the crowd somewhere.

Neita is glued to the tele. Like Gordon Nolan she knows Greg so well she can tell by watching him when he is in trouble and likely to get out. Certain tell-tale signs give him away when he is anxious or is getting too excited. If she is at the ground and it is not too noisy she will call out to him. If it is a game before a big crowd she will signal to him with her hands.

'I can see when he gets too adventuresome and uptight . . . I give him a sort of . . .' she waves her hands up and down . . . 'Which means calm down . . . In the early stages he is often tentative. I watch him on the tele when he plays interstate. He hangs his bat out and you can see it coming and I am here saying, 'Hit the thing.' And he hangs his bat out and is caught in the slips. I could wring his neck really and truly, I know he knows better.'

She is the one who needs to calm down now.

Greg approaches the crease. Frank Tyson says: 'Matthews scored 184 against Tasmania. It's not all over yet. He looks very determined.' Too right thinks Neita.

Meanwhile Jillian is in a dither. She wants to be at the ground in time to see Greg go on. It will be the first time she has seen him bat in a Test match. In the first innings he was already out when she got there. This morning she is sitting around the hotel pool enjoying the sun. Australian wickets are falling cheaply. Normally she gets ready to go out to the ground when Greg's team are two wickets down. She switches on the radio to check the score. Australia are four wickets down. It sends Jillian into a panic. She wants to get in position before Greg bats as she knows he will be looking for her and if she is not there it might put him off his game. Those other batsman had better do their bit.

She races back to her room. It is a hot day. She decides to put on a pair of shorts. It would turn out to be a bad decision. She rushes out of the hotel and grabs a cab to the ground. Wickets seem to be falling all over the place. Jillian is still in the cab when Greg goes out to bat.

He searches for her in the crowd but she is not in her designated position in the members' stand. Hang in there Greg.

On the television Keith Stackpole, the great Australian opener, is at the microphone with Frank Tyson watching Greg closely. He says: 'He has to watch the gap between bat and pad. He needs a big innings to boost his confidence. He was the best of the Australian fieldsmen. Put everything into his bowling. If enthuisasm counts for anything, he certainly deserves to score runs. He is quite a character. Some think he is more than that. Just what Australia needs at the moment.'

Ian Chappell takes over from Stackpole. The Australian team has not performed nearly as well as Chappell's team did. The eleven playing against New Zealand are very much a new look side. There is no Dennis Lillee, Greg Chappell, Rod Marsh or Kim Hughes in the side to give the young players confidence. Border is the only real veteran.

The new team is trying to build credibility. They have been to the Institute of Sport in Canberra and have talked about the new professionalism in an effort to rebuild the team. Chappell is of the old school who thinks all the sports psychology and all the other modern sports aids in the world will not make a Test cricketer. The Australian team under him were able to match it with anyone in the world. They never needed any of this airy fairy stuff. They were men who learnt their trade – where it counts – on the field – they never needed a sports psychologist for Christ's sake.

Chappell is not too impressed with the attitude of the Australians in the New Zealand Test. 'We heard a lot about the new professionalism. But we have not seen much evidence with the number of no balls etcetera bowled. It makes you wonder.'

Despite his misgivings about the Australian team in general, Ian Chappell is impressed with Greg's attitude early on in his innings. 'Matthews seems to have confidence in taking the strike so early.'

Frank Tyson chips in, 'He is playing every ball on its merits.' Greg appears to be thriving on the pressure.

Jillian is not. She has finally got to the ground. Greg is on eleven.

She tries to get into the members' area so that she can sit where Greg is expecting to see her. But the official on the gate knows his job. You can see him thinking, 'Women in shorts are not allowed into the members area young lady and don't think I am going to bend the rules because you say your sweatheart is out there batting.'

In desperation Jillian settles for a seat in the public section. She sits on her own down the front hoping Greg will spot her before he gets out. But how on earth will he see her in this crowd? He must be looking for her. The tension is killing her.

Things are pretty tense on the field. The New Zealand captain, Jeremy Coney, has the runs in hand to play with and is really putting the pressure on Greg. The New Zealand bowlers want to get him out and have a shot at the tail. They feel far more confident about dismissing Greg, the young whipper snapper, than Border, one of the most tenacious batsmen in the world.

The New Zealand pace and medium pace bowlers are unable to extract much from the pitch. Even the great Hadlee is not making much of an impression. Coney decides it is time to change tactics. He brings the off-spinner, Vaughan Brown, on. It is a good move by Coney. Greg with his offbreaks had been the most effective of the Australian attack. Coney places four close-in fieldsmen around Greg. They are poised for the catch. They are very close. If they were all at a party, Greg would be able to smell them. Let's see how he faces up.

New Zealand are working on Greg's nerves at every opportunity. He does not look all that comfortable against Brown. He is prodding about a bit. Greg takes a Brown delivery on the pads. The New Zealanders go up in the air and appeal enthusiastically.

'More in hope than anticipation,' says Richie Benaud, another ex-Australian captain turned cricket commentator, who is able to speak remarkably clearly through his nose. Benaud is aware of Greg's predicament. 'It is possible if he has a good innings,' Richie says, 'he won't be the eleventh man chosen but one of the first.'

Greg finally spots Jillian. From then on he steals moments throughout the game to stare at her. Somehow he seems more confident and self assured. Someone in the crowd near Jillian yells out, 'What is he staring at?' Jillian smiles to herself and just sits there.

The television screen shows Greg with the bat lying across his shoulders, a hand at each end. He rotates his body. This action was later to be part of a video clip set to the Hoodoo Gurus song 'Like Wow Wipe Out,' which was later put together by Channel 9 to capture the essence of Greg's inspiring eccentricity.

But Frank Tyson is not to know this. It just looks a little daft to him. 'Surely he does not need to warm up. It's sweltering out there.'

Whatever, it seems to be working. Greg is doing what the other Australian batsmen failed to do – put up a fight and support his captain. Greg is looking good and the runs are coming. Border is 51. Greg is 34. The commentators are already doing there best to tempt fate.

It is amazing how many batsmen get out the moment after an expert starts eulogising them. But Greg is the most interesting thing out there and there has to be sound with the pictures. Tony Greig makes his prophecy, 'If he is still there at the end of the day people will say he has earned his stripes as a Test batsman and competitor.'

The last thing Jeremy Coney and the other New Zealanders want is for Greg to establish himself. New Zealand people are very conservative. Greg is not their kind of guy. They desperately want to put this brash young man in his place – which they think is in the pavilion watching his teammates being bowled out. The New Zealanders do everything they can to maintain the pressure. They now have six men within ten metres of Greg's bat. 'They certainly fancy themselves against Greg Matthews,' Greig said.

The greater the adversity the greater the triumph. Greg maintains his poise and run rate. He makes his second half-century in Test cricket with a cut for three through point in the last over before tea.

While the players take drinks, Chappell has to fill in air time with chatter. Greg is the man everyone wanted to hear about. Chappell obliges, 'He might be among the first two or three picked for the next Test.' But he is not completely sold on the Matthews' style.

Greg thinks a Test wicket is a Test wicket no matter what the score is and it is something to be proud of and happy about. Although the New Zealanders had left Australia way behind, when Greg had taken Martin Crowe's wicket he had leapt in the air and punched it with delight. He showed more emotion in that moment than some cricket commentators display in three seasons. Crowe is greatness and Greg was suitably pleased to get his wicket. In fact he felt fantastic. Why not enjoy the moment? Why not savour it? Wow.

'He shows a lot of enthusiasm in the field,' Chappell said with a deadpan expression. 'I would like him to tone it down a bit though. Terrific if it is four or five for 70 but if its three or four for 300 perhaps he could tone that down. He is a great competitor and I wish him all the success.'

Chappell is a very knowledgeable cricket commentator and a fine interviewer, who as a commentator is able to talk without moving any facial muscles. If you talk to him in the flesh, he is relaxed, funny and incisive. On camera he has the sponteneity of an action replay. Producers have told him to lighten up. But it must be like telling Hilditch to stop hooking.

The screen flashes to be a delighted Greg shaking hands with an equally delighted Allan Border after Greg reached his 50. 'That sums it up,' Richie says. The camera flashes again to Greg and Border as their hands meet. Richie says, 'Boom . . . there it is.'

But there is a lot of work to be done before the boys can rest. 'He just can't get too carried away,' Ian Chappell says. 'Richard Hadlee is just the man to exploit any weakness.'

Greg is hit on the finger. He jumps around in pain. If the innings is to be truly great a broken bone does not go astray, what an achievement it would be to save Australia when badly wounded. Alas it seems to be alright. After a bit of capering about, Greg continues on from where he left off.

Like Chappell, Richie's long suit is not his ability to let his face express his emotions, but he can sense when something special is happening. 'Matthews is playing in his sixth Test match so you could really say he has only got through one series. This is an important day for him in his cricket career. He is following on from most wickets taken in the New Zealand first Innings. Brilliant fielding exhibition. And now he is sharing a partnership with his skipper.'

Matthews confidence and score continue to grow. Greg fiddles about with his bat on the field. On the television Stackie says,

'Border has given Greg Matthews a lot of confidence. Just as Matthews has instilled confidence in Border to let the young fellow do his own thing. He is certainly a little different . . . Today he walked to the wicket with a great deal of conviction. He gritted the teeth and has kept them fairly close together. With bat and pad, it has been a great performance.'

The crowd begins to chant. Greg is so mentally immersed in the task at hand when batting that he cannot really hear the crowd.

'It has been an innings of some character,' Keith Stackpole says. 'Let's hope Greg Matthews keeps his head down. In the last over we saw Allan Border hit that one for six. I hope he [Greg] does not try to follow suit . . .'

Stackie knows his man. Greg tries to sweep the ball out of the ground. Sometimes a six lifts the momentum of the batsmen. Greg is feeling solid and confident. But over-confidence often means trouble.

Greg does not quite get hold of the shot. He watches the ball fly into the air and Bruce Edgar race after it. It is going to be touch and go whether he reaches it. Greg does not move. He stares after the ball and thinks: 'Oh no. This is not fair. I have been given a chance and I am seeing the ball well. Don't catch it.'

Tong Greig said: 'That's going in the air down towards the fieldsman on the boundary . . . just over his head . . . Matthews wants to be a little careful of that one too. He has played so well. Taking chances at this stage could result in him losing his wicket.'

Stackie puts in his three cents worth. 'His heart would have been in his mouth as he played that sweep. Was not quite at the pitch of the ball and you see he does not even move as he waits to see if it is going to elude Bruce Edgar down there. For a change just a little bit of luck going the way of the Australians.'

Greg thinks, 'If I was bowling I would be very disappointed. If I was fielding there I would have got a hand to it. It was an important moment in the game. They need to break the partnership.'

But he survives and moves on to 85. The partnership is now worth 152. He plays clumsily at a ball which ricochets off his pad just in front of the New Zealand captain Jeremy Coney at silly point. A

commentator says, 'Greg Matthews has looked more vulnerable against the off-spinner.' Greg then plays a perfect defensive shot and the commentator says, 'That's better . . . A good safe shot.'

But you can't talk about cricket endlessly on tele. Tony Greig is always looking for something different to say. He settles for the traffic this time. 'The afternoon traffic is beginning to wind it's way home down the Ipswich Road I would say. They will get home in time, with a little bit of luck, to see these two chalking up a 100.'

Greg is on 86. Martin Snedden is bowling to two slips and a gully. Greg hits one nicely away over the square leg's head. The crowd around Jillian applauds madly. Greg's mum in the family home at West Ryde goes, 'Pst. Pst. Go the red. Go the red. Pst.' The balls goes into the boundary. Matthews joins Border on 90. Greg glances at the scoreboard. Border and Matthews partnership is now 150. They scored the runs in 270 minutes after facing 182 deliveries. They talk to one another. They reinforce each others' confidence and con- centration. They fill each others heads with the right thoughts, 'Come on let's do it . . . We must remember our responsibilities . . . Hustle . . . You are doing a great job.'

Greg is so close to his first Test century, yet the slightest mistake could intervene and keep the Test 100 in the fantasy basket. The nineties test a batsman's nerve. It is only a matter of centimetres from the centre of the bat to the edge and not far from the nearest fieldsman's hands. The walk to the pavilion is never longer than when the batsman is out in the nineties.

The nineties are the most trying time in this horribly frustrating sport. All can be going so well until the scoreboard rolls around to 90. Many a man changes from a fierce competitor to a tentative prodder. It is one thing to play for Australia, but to score a test 100. Once it is in the record books it is there forever. Ten runs away.

Tony Greig has been there. He says, 'Border has been in the nineties on numerous occasions before. Matthews hasn't. His top score of course is 75 in the first Test he ever played. It will be interesting to see how he handles the so called nervous nineties. I will tell you what Stackie, if he does get a 100, he is going to go berserk.'

Keith says: 'An interesting feature Tony is that Allan Border had 26 runs when Matthews came to the crease. He really has played well. Apart from playing a support role, he has not been afraid to hit the ball either. Matthews really deserves a three figure score beside his name. I only hope Allan Border does give him a little bit of guidance through the nineties. If he tries to get it the easy way . . . I hope Allan goes up and has a chat to him.'

The ABC commentator Jim Maxwell is not at the microphone. He is out and about in the ground. He sees Jillian sitting alone and goes up to her and says. 'Gee, Greg is doing well.'

'Yes', replies a nervous Jillian. The crowd overhears the conversation and puts two and two together and realises why Greg has been looking over in their direction so often. Everyone calls Maxwell 'Jim'. But Greg likes the sound of James and calls him that. So does Jillian. To the crowd he is that commentator from the ABC and Jillian is Greg's special friend and almost a celebrity. She is treated with new respect. They give her many a sideways glance.

Greg does not look too daunted by the nineties. He has a good attitude. He remembers the wisdom of the great Indian opener Sunil Gavaskar who reckons you should never look at the scoreboard. When you are in the nineties and you look your head changes. It's the same with the forties. Except for that peek at 90 Greg keeps his mind on the next ball. He reminds himself, 'Be positive. Be positive. Be positive. Don't freeze up. Be positive. Play each ball on its merits.'

He strikes the ball firmly into the ground. Mrs Matthews leans forward in her chair in front of the tele and goes, 'Pst pst pst. Go the red. Go the red. Pst . . . Come on Gregory Richard John.' she is trying to will the ball to the boundary. There is no third man and the ball makes its way to the fence. Mrs Matthews gets out of her chair to clap and holler. The four runs takes Greg to 94.

Sports commentators are masters at stating the obvious. Stackie is up there with the best of them. 'Greg Matthews is four runs closer to picking up a 100 in a test match,' he says. 'I would like to see a couple more of those.'

The crowd is tense and expectant.

Stackpole says, 'Eight runs off that over . . . I think you are going to see a happy man unbeaten on 94.'

Greig is commentating. 'He's up against the off-spinner now.

That's a little dangerous. Sweeps again ... this time it is to a fieldsman on the boundary. Just one to Greg Matthews. He keeps strike ... Needs just five runs. Third man has dropped down now. Two slips. Jeremy Coney is going to make him work a little harder for it ... That's hit nicely straight down the ground. Could have been four runs. Nice bit of fielding by Martin Snedden because that was hit with a lot of power. Greg Matthews showing he is not going to freeze up. He is going to play his shots if the ball is there to be hit. Gets the ball away to third man for one run. Just four runs short of his first 100 in Test cricket. Have a look at that he is starting to smile already. Don't count those chickens before they hatch.'

Keith Stackpole: 'Jeremy Coney has dropped that man down there to third man. He has saved six runs so far in this over.'

Greg is on 96. The field in place is two slips, a third man and a fine leg. Greg is on strike on 96. Border is on 92. Greg strokes the ball into a gap and moves to 97.

Neita has put off making that cup of tea. Jillian is beside herself. Members of the crowd have started talking to her. One old digger says, 'What do you reckon he will do when he gets his 100. You know what I think. I think he will come running over here like he did for his mum in Sydney.'

Jillian told Greg before the match, 'If you score 100 don't come running over to me and make a scene.'

'Sure. Sure,' Greg said, as if to say don't be so silly.

Tony Greig takes up the commentary. 'Greg Matthews is on strike facing the off-spinner ... He has had a few problems against the off-spinner ... Jeremy Coney knows that ... He is moving in a bit closer at silly point trying to put a bit more pressure on him. There is a man at deep square leg waiting for the lofted sweep shot ... Man at slip. Greg Matthews is very tense I would suggest ... Drives ... straight to the fieldsman ...'

The world outside is still happening. Many Australians are on the edge of their seat, but most of the world is oblivious to the drama at the Gabba. It is 4.54 pm in Brisbane and 5.54 in Sydney. The news must go on.

'We will be returning our Sydney and Melbourne viewers to their respective newses in six minutes time,' Tony Greig tells us.

But the news can wait. Greg walks down the wicket to talk to Allan Border. As he walks back he thinks, 'This over will be it. Be positive.'

In the stands Jim Maxwell takes his leave of Jillian. 'I think you two should have this moment together,' he says.

Tony Greig takes over the commentary. Vaughan Brown moves in. He bowls a full delivery outside off stump.

'He has gone for it,' Greig says forgetting to use his lower registers. 'It's down the ground . . , this could be six . . . it is . . . his first 100 and is he happy . . . It's a beautiful six . . . Well . . . isn't he enjoying it.'

As soon as Greg hit the ball he knew he had his 100. He ducks his head, slams the bat in the ground and started running towards the stand where Jillian is sitting. He jumps in the air. Blows kisses to Jillian in the stand. Draws M for Mumma with his finger in the air for Neita in front of the tele at home. He goes back to shake hands with Border. In the stands Jillian is so happy she is in tears. At home Neita Matthews does a highland fling. Her boy has done it and the whole neighbourhood can hear it.

'Nothing could be better than this,' Talking Heads.

Greg does not realise it is a six at first. He goes back to the crease, turns to the New Zealand keeper and says, 'Was that a four or a six.' He does not hear the reply and looks at the scoreboard which reads: 'G.R.J. Matthews 103.'

Stackpole has not had a chance to get a word in. Finally Greg stops gushing. Stackpole says, 'I think we are lucky he stayed on the ground . . . a tremendous effort by the off-spinner . . . I think Tony it is the first time ever I have seen a fellow going for his 100 run the other way when he hit the ball. Normally you see them running around looking for the one or the two or the three, but he knew it was right off the middle of the bat. It was going to go over that boundary rail. What a way to get it? Six runs.'

There must be some relevant fact and figure worth dredging up to mark the moment. There is. 'There have not been too many players who have done that over the years,' Stackpole says, 'in fact I think there is only one player that has done it twice in the history of Test cricket and that was Ken Barrington.'

The 100 runs came from 179 balls.

Tony Greig says, 'Settle down son you have to be there at the close

of play. What an innings it has been. I just hope now he has got his three figures he gets back his concentration.

Can't get too carried away. 'A lot of work to be done yet by the Australians,' Stackpole says.

Greg lets the final ball of the over go through to the keeper and Greig says, 'He let that one go through to the keeper. A good over for Matthews and Australia. His third first class century.'

Border does not say anything for a while and then, 'I have got a lot of faith in you Greg.'

When the cricket does give way to the news, the new is still cricket. On Sydney's Channel 9 the matey commentator, Mike Gibson, says, 'Border and Matthews combined to give Australia a fighting chance.' Highlights of the game flash on the screen. We see Border belt one. Gibson says: 'This one from Border ... right out of the ground ... One from the skipper deserves one from the kid – a magic moment as Matthews smashes a six for his century.' The segment finishes with Border getting his 100 and Frank Tyson saying, 'What a revival this has been. Worthy of Billy Graham.'

It must be time for the weather.

THE MORNING AFTER

There is a formula for making an athlete into a marketable commodity. Three things are essential: an interesting personality, or the appearance thereof, heroic sporting performances and the backing of the marketing machines. It is all a matter of how the public sees you. Greg Chappel was seen as too cool in the emotional, not hip sense, Allan Border as too dour, Greg Norman, the golfer, as someone who chokes and Adair Stephenson, a rower, excels at an obscure sport and is not seen. All are champions, but none match the appeal of Greg.

In March 1986 Bob Simpson said, 'Research has shown that Greg is a very marketable bloke. His attraction is that he not only appeals to the younger generation but to the mums as well.'

Since then Greg has done a number of promotions, and talks and has been used to sell Diet Coke and the United Permanent building society. The Liberal party wanted to use him to woo the young hip vote. Through shrewd promotion John Bertrand and John Newcombe have managed to stay in the public eye and mind long after they retired from their sports. If an athlete is publicly portrayed as a cult hero for a few years, he or she will be imbedded in the minds of the public forever and will become a millionaire. 'Greg Matthews has a chance of doing that,' Lynton Taylor said.

Lynton Taylor is the managing director of PBL Marketing, the company that promotes and markets international cricket in Australia. PBL is associated with the Kerry Packer controlled, Australian Consolidated Press. Taylor knows what sells, including personalities.

Greg plays in a sport where personalities are few and far between, but as in affairs of the heart, personality is not everything. PBL's market research shows that Allan Border was the most popular figure in the Australian team in 1986. Despite Border's greatness as a player, Greg is a far more attractive marketing package. 'Greg is a personality, people talk about him', Lynton Taylor said. 'He stands out as a character and gets a lot of attention in the papers. Given another good year, mind you he did not play so well at the end of last season [1985-86], my research suggests that Greg Matthews could be number one.'

Greg has had a marketable personality for several years, but it was not until he really performed on the field that the marketing machines could capitalise on his personality and Greg Matthews the eccentric cricketer could become a cult hero. He became the subject of a '60 Minutes' segment, a Greg Matthews' video was made, he was written about outside the sports pages, has appeared in advertisements and had this book written about him. American athletes never feel they have really made it until they feature in a national advertising campaign.

But it all starts with the performance on the field, on the court or on the course. 'What made his popularity were his performances', Lynton Taylor said. 'If Greg has a bad season, is dropped from the Australian team and becomes just another also-ran in the NSW team, he will be quickly forgotten.'

I asked a friend of mine and long-time cricket follower, Peter Womack, what he thought of Greg. 'I like him because he is good', Womack said. 'When the chips are down, he knocks a ton and he seems an interesting guy. But as soon as he gets hit around and gets a succession of ducks, I would lose interest, same as I would in any sportsman.'

By scoring that First Test century against New Zealand Greg had put in an heroic performance and the critics eulogised him. Bill O'Reilly began his column with Shakespeare. 'There is a tide in the affairs of men which taken at the flood leads on to fortune.'

'No young cricketer of my experience has better portrayed the great poet's inspiring thought than the young Western Suburbs all-rounder who has pounded his way into the hearts of Australian

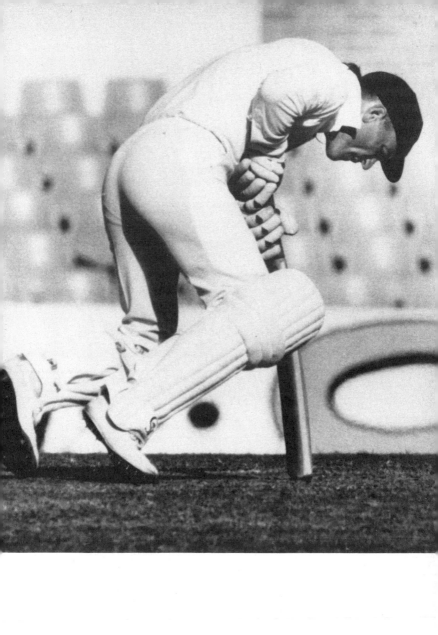

followers especially those Sydneysiders who have seen him emerge from the grey-blue distance into the limelight of topline cricket publicity in the short time since his first-class career began . . . Isn't it funny how a young man can suddenly drag himself from the hurly burly and come striding forth with a charm that no one can possibly deny?'

'A few days ago and the average cricket expert thought Matthews was lucky to be included in the 12 to line up in Brisbane for the First Test, and the majority of those were quite certain that he was there to fill the 12th man position – thinking that utility man Simon O'Donnell who performed fairly well in England, would beat him to the punch for a place in the team. As his reward for one of the most inspiring portrayals of guts in a crisis in the Gabba Test, Matthews' magnificent century against the odds has made his name a household cricket word – because he behaved in precisely the manner all Australians hope a young favourite will adopt when the chips are down . . . he can be quite certain that the selectors when they meet around the table tomorrow will make the immediate observation: There's Border and Matthews . . . who are the next ten.'

Richie Benaud agreed. 'When the team for the Sydney Test is chosen next week he will be number two, with only skipper Allan Border ahead of him. Such was the devastating effect he had on the match, the New Zealanders, the selectors, spectators and his own teammates . . . It was a remarkable performance . . . When I had played the same number of Tests I had done nothing of this quality . . . Alongside Border he has looked a splendid Australian cricketer.'

The headlines were equally flattering: 'Allan, Greg Show 'em How, A Gallant Greg Shows the Way, Brave Greg, Our Boy Greg, Greg the Destroyer etc.'

The only down side of that occasion was that our hero was magnificent in defeat. But Greg fixed that. He started a match-winning 100 against India at the MCG on Boxing Day to steer Australia to a draw on a pitch which Border described as one of the worst three first-day wickets he had played on. Greg moved from 59 to 100 with only his good friend and pace bowler Dave Gilbert to help him.

'Greatest innings that 100 against India. Going out to bat I was thinking, "Well I am going to have to slog here," I saw the video of it and I can remember from the first ball I got a single and just felt different . . . It was just my day. It is a hard thing to put down. Basically there is no real formula, it was just my day. I watched myself when I was batting with Dave Gilbert and he walked past and I can remember he said something to me and none of it was registering . . . I knew where I was going. I knew what I was doing I knew what I had to do. It just happened. It was amazing. I looked back and I think I must find a way to tap it. I must find a way to tap into it.'

During that innings Greg controlled the game in a way he never had before. He came in to bat when Australia had lost five wickets. Jillian: 'It really was just right that day. I new if Dave Gilbert could just hang in there Greg would get his century. I knew it.'

Greg controlled the strike. After facing the first four or five balls of every over, he seemed to be always able to hit a two or a four and keep the strike and shield Gilbert. 'Dave Gilbert', Greg said, 'I will never forget what he did for me that day. I would have liked to have given him a hug but I know he does not like it so I just have him a pat on the back and walked away.'

Everyone was impressed with the innings. Dirk Wellham said he never realised Greg could play so well. O'Reilly said Matthews had turned on one of the greatest moral lessons that cricket had ever taught him. 'He embraces all the qualities that we admire in our heroes who have graced our cricket fields since this country began . . . Matthews is a hero to every young Australian I have yet to meet. I am on his side. I congratulate all those kids who beat me smartly to the point.'

Border was also won over. 'He's one fellow who never says die; he tended to keep everyone else going when the match at times appeared to be slipping from our grasp. It is pleasing to have him doing this and playing such good cricket.'

Matthews followed this up with some good performances in the one-dayers. On 12 January 1986, Australia was on top of the one-day competition and Greg was seen as responsible for the revival. The headlines reflected the general feeling. 'Babes teach mentors how to win at cricket . . . Matthews – he's just magic.'

But it takes a long time before a personality becomes imbedded in the public consciousness. As Greg said at the end of 1986, 'It takes more than one season to make the man.'

Lynton Taylor knows that fame is all relative. 'From my experience in TV, it is amazing the number of people who think they have it made, after they have been the star of a soapie or something for a year and have had plenty of exposure, been written up in the newspapers. Then they do something else for a while and a few months after it is finished people don't recognise them. We do immediate recall research and find that the public don't register their names.'

Lynton Taylor says that while Greg's eccentricity has contributed to his popularity, he should restrain himself from going too far. 'Someone like Greg has a lot of potential, particularly with his appeal to the kids, but he has to be careful that he does not go over the top. Cricket appeals to a terrific cross section of age groups. But if you are over the top people won't relate to you.'

But you get the feeling that Greg knows where his sponsorship bread is buttered. 'He's toned it down a lot', Oaksie said. 'He used to brag. Sledge people . . . He gives people more of a go these days. In the old days if he did not like somebody he would not give them any time and would tell them exactly what he thought of them . . . Now he is somebody. He can't do that in public . . He knows if a drunk comes up to him and Greg says a few words to him that guy will think he is a great guy and tell his mates. I have seen him talk to guys patiently I would have told to piss off. I guess if you do that when you are a personality it gets you a bad name.'

Neita said, 'More people like Greg now than don't these days.'

Dave Gilbert said many of his fellow cricketers wished they could perform as well as Greg in the on-field personality stakes. Clowning and being the extrovert on the field can't be forced. If it isn't natural it shows and looks stupid. The English spinner, John Emburey, said to Greg in England, 'I wish I could behave the way you do on the cricket field. You can relate to the crowds and express your feelings.' And get to do television commercials.

All of this begs the question, is Greg putting on an act designed to make him a more marketable and thus richer personality?

Bob Aitken, who first knew Greg as an eleven-year-old, thinks

154

Allan Border, Dave Gilbert, Greg Matthews

Greg has deliberately played up his eccentricities so he would become a personality player. He thinks Greg is very cunning and is in many ways similar to Tony Greig, with whom Greg gets on very well. Greig used to play to the crowd, has marketed himself well, done television commercials, got a job in insurance through cricket and is a commentator for Channel 9. Greg is hoping that something will come up for him through cricket for life after. He is not sure what but has his eyes well and truly open.

Maybe Aitken and Greg never saw eye to eye and Aitken is likely to be a little cynical about Greg. Dave Gilbert and Greg are good mates. On tour they share the same room most of the time. 'There is a real method to his madness', Gilbert said. 'He has a calculating mind. He has a reason for doing what he does. He knows very well that people encourage the services of someone who is different like Greg Matthews or Mark Jackson [the VFL player]. People always talk about them. Greg Matthews sees that as an important facet of marketing Greg Matthews. You don't see a game where he won't do something different for the crowd'

Cricket is a great vehicle for public exposure. A little personality goes a long way. Even a fringy player with a personality like Michael Whitney has, through cricket, been able to star in a beer commercial, work as a radio broadcaster and work for Powerplay, the company that markets the Swans.

Whitney admires Greg's lack of inhibitions on the field. You get the sense he would like to share the Greg Matthews image. He felt alienated when he first started playing Shield before Greg came along as he too enjoys expressing his feelings on the field. Unlike some of the other players he gives the American basketball slapping handshake whether Greg is there or not, and like Greg, puts in a 110 per cent effort during games.

If Whitney had had the consistent good Test performances on the field he would have been a personality player, no question. He looks good, is articulate and outspoken, is approachable, has a mane of curly hair, wears an earring and is well aware of his image. But he has not yet managed to become a regular Test player.

Whitney considers Greg a friend. 'Everyone thinks he is putting on

Michael Whitney

a show. Maybe he is to a certain extent. But he has always been bobbing around, always a little outrageous. He has never swum with the school.' I told him what Aitken and Gilbert had said. 'He has always been that way, but probably in his own mind he knew that if the time and place was right he could capitalise on it and that is what he has done. He is certainly not lacking in the grey matter department . . . I love him. I have a lot of respect for the guy as a person. His attitude to people is right. I have been out with him and people hassle him and he understands it comes with the territory and he handles it. He takes it easy.'

Has Greg changed with his success? Brother Peter says not really, but he has become more confident because of the attention he has received. Rubbing shoulders with celebrated characters, including the Prime Minister, has given him a boost or maybe justified the confidence he already had. 'Sometimes he comes across as arrogant', Peter said, 'but I think it is just his confidence. He was always confident as a kid.'

Neita thinks Greg is freer now because people who would not accept him two years ago will now that he is more successful. Maybe it is a matter of perspective. Some journalists say Greg used to be one of the most approachable cricketers, but after the summer of 1985-86 they say he tends to walk past them with his big loud sunglasses on and be far more offhand in his dealings with the press. Greg courts and enjoys the attention but guards his privacy and time with Jillian. He is constantly being inundated with offers to star in film, endorse a product, to speak at a dinner. It can wear anyone down.

'Next season [1986-87], to make my job easier, I'm not going to need this hassle of people coming and gadding about a movie.

'It's extra weights, it's extra responsibility. It's a little funky, it's a little too deep.'

Doesn't being a Test cricketer imply other responsibilities?

'I am aware of that. I sign more autographs than most people. I accept that as part of my job. But I am not perfect. Enough is enough sometimes.'

Time is something Greg never seems to have enough of. He spends it carefully. Even dear friends don't get much time. Oaksie once rang Greg, after he had not seen him for nine months.

"Oaksie, Oaksie how are you going? . . . Good to hear from you . . . What are you up to?"

Oaksie suggests they get together.

"Love to great idea. Let me see. Tomorrow's out. Friday's out. Weekend I am busy. Look I will give you call ok . . . Good to hear from you."

But when they do catch up Greg will go out of his way to make Oaksie know they are still close. 'He is my friend and that is an important word in my vocabulary. I don't use it lightly.' He will fob off fans and attractive autograph hunters so he can talk to his man Oaksie. 'He works overtime to make me feel that we still have got it. He always brings up things we did in England to make me feel good and welcome. I feel like saying Greg you don't need to do this. I will still be your friend. He does not need to do it.'

One time Oaksie was sitting with Greg's brothers Peter and Ian during a one-day game. Greg walked off the field after scoring one not out. Oaksie walked over to the gate where Greg walked off the field and yelled out above the general din, 'Well done Greg. Red ink.' Red ink was their code for not out. Greg did not seem to hear. Oaksie went and sat down. Next thing he knew Greg came bounding up and gave him a kiss on the cheek and said: 'Good to see you Oaksie.' He had picked Oaksie's voice and had just wanted to show he cared.

Jillian says Greg has not changed a great deal. 'When you go out its great for free drinks. People are always buying us free drinks . . . He does not relax as much as he did before. People are always watching him. I think he is more subdued. Maybe it is added responsibility . . . A bit flamboyant in the way he dresses and stuff. Very well mannered and very polite to women. Can't do enough for me. See how he treats his mother. Treats everyone pretty well. Except yobbos who have had too much to drink . . . We are really going to want our privacy if it keeps going. I don't think anyone else has had this much publicity.'

HUSTLE

Getting time with Greg Matthews, happy home owner, multi-media hero, advertising personality, physiotherapy patient, supportive lover and Test cricketer is something to be valued. It took me ten days to pin him down for a final crucial interview. We had agreed to meet on a Thursday. I was sitting by the phone when tragedy struck.

'I'm sorry to do this to you', he said over the phone. 'I need to have this x-ray done . . . The physiotherapist wants it . . . this is my life, my job!'

What about tonight?

'I have got to see Jillian. She needs me right now. She will kill me if I don't go and see her tonight. I will speak to her to see if it's alright for you to come over. I'll ring you tonight one way or another.' Cheque's in the mail. I thought of Oaksie and Dave Gilbert.

By Sunday I had heard nothing. I was getting desperate. I rang Greg again and tried the Matthews' hustle approach. I told him that this book was my life at the moment and I needed to see him, urgently. Surely he could spare me an hour. The approach worked on the master. He sounded sympathetic and said with an ounce of luck he would fit me in the next day, if possible.

Even though it was not the cricket season, Greg, had got himself into a whirl of activity. His life had been full of filming for TV ads, buying a house in Paddington and dealing with builders, lawyers and real estate agents, helping Jillian at her fabric printing and design shop, the odd business lunch, cricket training and sessions with the physiotherapist at Sutherland. 'Bear with me', he said. 'I am trying to keep my head together.'

Jillian and I agreed that Greg is a drama queen. For him, life is always a run chase on the last session of play on the last day of the deciding Test, with nine wickets down and Greg the wounded batsman at the crease facing the fastest bowler the world has ever seen. The decision on which house to buy had kept Greg awake at nights wondering whether he had done the right thing. The week he stood me up, the running drama had been learning the lines for a 30-second commercial.

But there was a tunnel at the end of the light. It looked as though he would have some time the following Monday. Greg spent the morning filming for a Diet Coke ad. He was picked up at 6.30 am and was on the go until lunchtime. He had to be at the physio's at 6 pm or 7 pm, the time changed. But he might just fit me in in the afternoon. He promised to call.

Greg was not the only busy soul that afternoon. I was working with my Penguin editor, John Curtain, who had come to Sydney to discuss the book. He thought it would be nice to meet Greg. He knew I was *desperate* to see Greg.

The phone rang. 'Greg here. I'm home. I can see you now.'

I told him John would quite like to meet him.

'No disrespect, but the place is a mess . . . We know you, so if you see the place like it is, that's ok. But we don't know Mr Curtain . . . Jillian wouldn't appreciate it.'

Ok ok we understand.

The night before I had been burgled, the meeting with John Curtain had already been interrupted by a visit from the police, a window repair man and a search for stolen briefcases in the back streets of Paddington. When we finally got down to business we decide the book neeeds an 'up' ending focussing on Greg's last great season. Hopefully I can get sufficient information in this last interview to do this. We hastily wrap up the meeting so I can see Greg. We plan to meet later, hopefully with Greg, and I head over to Greg's Elizabeth Bay apartment thinking of the previous cricket season and what it had meant to Greg.

Greg's career really took off after the 100 against New Zealand at the Gabba. He scored centuries for NSW against Tasmania and New

Zealand. In the Second Test against New Zealand he scored 50 and 32 and took vital wickets in each innings. Greg played the best innings of his life in the second Test against India when he almost singlehandedly controlled the game and scored 100 not out.

In the finals of the one-day series against India Greg was declared Man of the Series. When Australia went to New Zealand Greg was in demand. His captain, Allan Border, wanted him in the side for the First Test if at all possible. 'Matthews may not be fully fit', Border said, 'but it would take something extraordinary for us to leave him out. He is so very important to us and as long as he feels okay he plays.'

So there was plenty for us to talk about. 'How do you like the shirt', Greg says shortly after I walk in. 'I bought it today.'

It's not me. I tell him so.

'It's too up-market for you. You like the scruffy look ... It's sensaysh. A winner.'

Greg fires off the next question. 'Did you see my ad on the television over the weekend.'

Greg makes a couple of calls about a contract for an advertisement and one other business call. 'I don't want to cause any waves or anything but the contract was supposed to be sent over priority paid and it should be here and it's not ... I don't want to sound like a frustrated human being ... Well if you say its on its way ... we will talk again at 10 pm tonight ok ... Gotta go ... I have someone with me.'

Next phone conversation. 'It is amazing the number of people who have come up to me and said how do you spell your name. It's got two 't's. Someone spelt my name wrong. It looks particularly sloppy because I have signed it correctly above ... Can you do anything about it .. I would have thought with all the money they had spent they would want to get it right.' End of conversation.

We sit down. He gets me a beer. I realise the bag with my spare tapes has been stolen in the burglary. I don't have any with me. I tell Greg, he offers to let me tape over one of his. But a bit of hustle is in order. 'You gotta get more organised Roland.'

The first question is about his First Test 100 against New Zealand. He was caught in the slips off a delivery from Richard Hadlee for 115 after thinking he had the ball covered. 'I really was so disappointed when I got out that time. I did not go home and tell my mates I had made a century. We lost. It was terrible. I really thought I had the chance to do something great for Australia that day.' During the innings he had played confidently, he was not playing and missing. He could not see why he could not do the seemingly impossible and bat through the next day's play with his captain, Allan Border, who finished with 152 not out, and save the match. 'I could have done it', he said.

Greg says it is more important to him that Australia win than he succeeds as an individual. The point of playing the game is to win and if you don't there is nothing to get excited about. Besides, everyone in the team is disappointed, tense and nervous and unlikely to have a good time. Greg also gets a huge kick out of seeing his friends in the team doing well. He is just as happy when Murray Bennett gets wickets as when he does.

And if something positive happens on the field, the physical contact is useful. Greg makes a point of saying that he likes the touching because it is good for the team and has nothing to do with his sexual preference which is above suspicion.

'I am not a homosexual ... I'm not a poofter ... The touching keeps the momentum going, it keeps people in touch. Makes everyone in the team part of the individual's success. Builds team unity.'

The next subject on the agenda is: How is cricket good for the character? Greg makes it sound better than Sunday School. 'It teaches you to take the good with the bad, accept the umpire's decision, be patient, get on with people, be humble, because everyone fails sometimes, be generous and trust your teammates.'

Throughout a match, players are under the microscope while under pressure. It brings out the best or the worst in them. 'It has made me a better human being', Greg says. 'What have I learnt? – I have learnt that I have good fighting qualities and don't lie down and die when the going gets tough.'

Everything seems to be going well with my interview, at last. Greg is feeling relatively relaxed, seems to be coming up with great little

insights. The last chapter will get done ok. There is a sense of urgency, but not negatively so. Greg treats me as a fellow team member.

As always he is full of suggestions and hustle. Whenever we get off the track or one of us goes out of the room Greg stops the tape. 'You have got to conserve it', he said. If I think of something, he will say, 'Better write it down.' He even seems to have my financial interests at heart. When I say I am not sure if I have received any money for a project I was working on, he said, 'You have got to get on to it . . . Do you know what this could be costing you . . . Ring your agent.'

Right.

'Tomorrow morning.'

When he thinks it is time to get back on the job: 'Let's go . . . Next question . . . How is the tape going?'

It had stopped. Tragedy. Flat batteries?

'Why don't you get some?' Greg said. No cash.

'Here's a blue swimmer', Greg says as he hands me $10 . . . 'You have got to get more organised.'

I race out, get the batteries and return. The tape still does not work.

'You have gotta get more organised. You could be interviewing the Queen and this could be your only chance.'

All of a sudden Greg has to get to the physio by 6 pm. I thought he had said 7 pm. 'It was definitely 6 pm', Greg says. We are in Elizabeth Bay in the heart of the city. I agree to take Greg to the physio at Sutherland, 40 minutes drive away to the south, if I can get a tape recorder that works. We head out the door.

In the lifts Greg says, "What do you think of this. A mirror to check yourself out on the way out."

He looks at himself carefully, fiddles with his hair, seems happy and says, 'Sensaysh,' with a smirk on his face.

We jump in the car and head off to Paddington, where I am staying. I am driving, Greg is in charge of motivation and tactics, in other words he is a shocking backseat driver, just as Oaksie had said. We approach a light that threatens to turn red. 'Come on gotta get this light', Greg says. 'It's an important one . . . Well done. You can be

166

stuck there for five minutes you know . . . I am really excited about buying this house . . .' I am really excited about making the lights and look forward to another chance to prove myself.

But being on Greg's team has its problems. You can't step out of line. The following day someone from the *Mirror* newspaper in Sydney rang me up and asked about the book. I tried to point out what an exciting project it was for about an hour and hung up. The eight paragraph story portrayed me in a way that did not fit my self image, but it was no big deal. A bit of a laugh.

A few days later Greg called. A friend answered the phone. 'I need to talk to Roland urgently.'

I was not home.

'Get him to call me the moment he walks through the door.'

Sounded important. I rang him and he goes on about the *Mirror* article as though it threatens his peace of mind.

It's no big deal.

'It is. Think about who you are talking too. Think about. Think about it . . . Gotta go.' He was not amused.

Ten minutes later I ring him back. The problem, it turns out, is that the story had been accompanied by a photo of Greg with Hazel Hawke. It had prompted speculation about Greg's politics.

'It creates a hassle for me. I have to ring up six people and say this and that to them. Think about it . . . Did you read todays *Telegraph.*'

What has it got to do with the *Mirror?*

'The Telegraph article was an outrageous article . . . About me and politics. Read the *Telegraph.*' We don't exactly agree to disagree, but we leave it at that. The story in the *Telegraph* said that the Liberal Party thought they needed someone like Greg to win the youth vote. Oh no. Now I understand the lack of amusement.

Back in the car Greg says he has five newspaper interviews slotted in for the next day. They are the hand that feeds the public image which does not exist without publicity. All of which makes people pay the money you make to appear in advertisements. It does not make sense to bite that hand.

Greg treats friendship very seriously. Saying someone is a friend to Greg is like conferring a knighthood. 'I call Dave Gilbert a friend,

Greg Matthews with Hazel Hawke

something I do not do lightly . . . I call Michael Whitney a friend, something I do not do lightly. . .'

We arrive at my house. Greg inspects it. Notices a deadlock is not on and a toilet needs flushing. He gives me his report. I am more interested in the other tape recorder. It does not work. Greg makes sure.

'You have gotta get more organised', he says.

I arrange to pick up another one at the *Eastern* (Sydney Morning) *Herald* offices. We are set to go. I ask him if he likes Bob Marley. 'I do, but not this afternoon'. We settle for Talking Heads.

We set off. When we are out the door, Greg points out that the living room curtain is not drawn. I rectify that. Back in the car things are not going smoothly. I have no sense of direction and have never been to the *Eastern Herald* at night. It is not where it should be. We circle around. Greg gives me some directions even though he does not know where we are going.

We circle around again. I still can't find the offices.

'You don't know where you are', says Greg. 'You have to get more organised.'

Things are looking ridiculously grim. If I don't get to interview Greg tonight I will be away behind schedule and who knows when I will be able to pin him down again. I know the offices are very close to where we are so I decide to ring up and get directions. Greg keeps the pressure on the opposing interviewer.

'Where are you going?' he says.

'I will be back in two minutes', I reply.

I find a public phone. Disaster. The mouthpiece of the phone has been ripped off. I wander around hoping to find a well informed stranger. I am about to give up when I stumble over the *Eastern Herald* offices. I feel relieved. On top of the world.

I run in, pick up a tape recorder. Go outside and wonder where Greg and car are. I feel it is all out of control. I find them. The plan is that I will ask the questions while Greg drives. He immediately starts assessing the car.

'The brakes grab, the steering is heavy and there is something wrong with third gear. It's a shocker.'

Normally when you interview someone for any length of time, you start off with a bit of general chit chat, ask a question to get things rolling and the conversation develops from there. The conversation is kept on track with the odd question.

Often it helps to make a few statements which stimulate the person you are talking to into saying something. Not with Greg. You ask him a question, he considers it and answers it. End of section. You ask another question and the same thing happens. Sometimes Greg clicks, gets rolling, has perceptive insights and the whole thing rolls along nicely. Other times . .

Back in the car I run out of question and the interview runs out of steam. I decide it is time for a general question. It should not be too hard for Greg to think of something, after all he has had quite a season. Mike Coward wrote in the *Sydney Morning Herald,* 'Since November he has scored three Test centuries, taken wickets, held breathtaking catches, fielded as if there was no tomorrow, inspired others with his deeds and deep sense of commitment, and won the respect of so many people in the world of cricket.'

I think Greg should be contributing something without what can be at times excruciating prodding, so I ask, 'Can you think of any interesting incidents which happened either in New Zealand or in Australia after you scored your Test century.'

Greg, usually the master of spontaneity, thinks about it for about 15 seconds. 'No.' Right we have dealt with that area.

I try the philosophical theory approach and rave on with some rubbish about cricket being a metaphor for life or some such thing. It was a bit like when a journalist asked Gough Whitlam a long winded question at the Canberra Press Club. The question went something like: 'When you were in power you said the essence of politics was conflict. We now have a Prime Minister who is talking consensus.' . . . Some lengthy passages from the French philosopher, Rousseau, were quoted and the question finished with . . . 'In the light of the Rousseauian notion of politics and your conflict theory, how do you reconcile that with the consensus politics of today?'

'Too deep for me', Gough said. To my question, Greg said: 'What?'

Anyway we need to stop to buy some chocolate bars. Greg pulls over. I fumble for money.

The traffic is banking up.

'Jeesus', Greg says as he hands me another blue swimmer.

I take the money and say thanks.

Greg says, 'Go go go.'

I think, 'Hustle hustle', and race to the shop. When I find the car after completing my errand Greg is at a service station calmly buying some cigarettes.

Back in the car I tell Greg how I try and use the Matthews approach to life in the surf. Surfing has been receiving more and more publicity, thousands of young people now dream of being a world champion surfer rather than a Test cricketer. Their heroes are champions like Tom Carroll and Mark Richards. Men such as Rod Marsh, Greg Chappell and Dennis Lillee do not excite. Greg might still be the kind of guy they could relate to. Anyway the surf is full of these aggressive would-be World champs and to get a wave you have to be in there hustling with the best of them. Even when there are only two people out there on a cold, blowy day, the competition for waves is as intense as for any Test match wicket. After spending a bit of time with Greg I decided to apply the Matthews' approach to surfing. So now when I surf I say to myself, 'Hustle ... hustle ... be positive ... Come on ... Let's do it ... Think about it.'

Greg seems to enjoy the story, smiles and says, 'Really'. But he is distracted by someone going round a roundabout too slowly. He shakes his head and says, 'Bad driving ... That's bad driving.' I would hate to drop a catch off Greg's bowling.

It's time to get back to cricket. Greg was named NSW Cricketer of the Year in 1986 after he took 31 first class wickets at an average of 24.42 and scored 890 runs at an average of 52.35.

Greg impressed more people than mere cricketing award judges. The already legendary Indian opener Sunil Gavaskar, who has scored more runs in Tests than any other player, said in an interview that Greg was the best thing that had happened to Australian cricket for years. 'Matthews is a joker and superstar', Gavaskar said. 'He would be a sensation wherever he plays ... He would be magic in India ... From what I've seen he is a much better batsman than bowler at the moment. He plays straight and correct and he applies the principles of playing himself in. He's an excellent runner between the wickets and has adapted to the one-day game. As a bowler, he has suffered perhaps because he is not the number one spinner for Australia. But he bowls with a nice loop and could develop into a very good Test spin bowler. He is so enthusiastic . . . He is the ideal team player.'

We arrive at the physiotherapists. Greg is greeted enthusiastically by everyone there and seems to thrive on the attention. Greg introduces me to the physio, 'This is Errol.' Errol Alcott is the Australian team physiotherapist and will be travelling with them to India.

'This is a friend of mine Roland Fishman . . . He is doing a book about me.' He disappears to talk to a secretary.

Greg takes his new shirt off. Underneath is a blue singlet with Fitness Network written on the front. He lies on his stomach while an ultra-sound machine is strapped to his shoulder. A towel slips off. He asks me to put it on him. I do.

'I hate this', he says.

It must be nice to just lie there?

'But my mind is racing',

The physio starts working on Greg's shoulder. Greg wants everything to be done just right. Anything less than 100 per cent is just not good enough. I start talking to the physio about this and that.

'You should not be talking', Greg tells Errol 'you have to give me 100 per cent. Come on.'

Greg does some repetition exercises standing against the wall. He has to do the exercise 12 times and repeat the routine eight times. When he gets to the final repetition it is hard work. Greg's face puffs up with the exertion, the veins bulge, the breathing is deep, the eyes are all scrunched up and the audience of two wills him on. He has the intensity of a man lifting for gold at the Olympic Games.

The next set of weights are on the table. They are the most difficult. The weights are held in a leather casing and look like a small pillow. For the wall exercise, the ends of the casing are connected and the weights fit snuggly around the hand. The weights for the lying down exercise are not bound.

'These weights don't feel right', Greg says.

Greg Matthews and Geoff Lawson

'They are heavier', Errol says.

'They are not right. I know I am going to be struggling on the eighth set. I want it to be right.'

'You want me to tape it together?'

'That would be sensaysh.'

Greg gets to the eighth set.

Before the final lift Greg psyches himself up. 'Good luck Mo . . . Let's do it. If you can get through this you are a legend.'

Where did this Mo come from? Greg is a card and loves playing 500 during breaks in play. One season he kept calling misere. He says it was because he had the cards but I am sure it was at least partly because he wanted to be at the centre of the game. The name stuck and when Ace, Imran Kahn, played for NSW he pronounced Misere, Mosere. The nickname became Mo.

While Greg is pumping away on his back, the strain is again written all over his body. He grips the side of the bed. The physio says, 'How are the muscles feeling?'

No response.

He asks again. Again no response. 'We can't disturb the concentration', Errol says. It is probably like the cocoon of concentration Greg Chappell entered when batting.

Greg gets through the set. He looks pleased with himself. I feel like cheering. 'I did 14 . . . It was not all quality, but I did it.'

'You should not do more than I say', Errol says. Greg looks hurt.

Greg has just bought his house in Paddington. He treats the exercise with all the seriousness of a Test match. Errol's father, Brian, has just bought a house in Paddington. He comes into the surgery, Greg is introduced and immediately starts talking about buying Paddington houses. They compare notes discussing; backyard access, knocking down walls and comparative real estate values and bargains. Errol's father leaves and Greg says, 'Maybe Jillian and I can come and see your house and maybe get some ideas for our place?'

Brian says, 'Anytime.'

Back in the car the discussion turns to the Sharjaz tour. Before the tour began Greg was doubly excited because he had been appointed third selector. Jillian rang to give him the good news.

'I was really stoked', Greg said at the time, 'national selector that's a big rap man . . . It's a bit of added responsibility and I hope I can handle it.'

In the *Daily Telegraph* Neil Harvey wrote that Matthews should be made vice-captain. Greg the fringe player and personality has become an established part of the Test world.

Greg is obviously captain material. He possess a valuable organ for the task – a fine cricketing brain. Gordon Nolan did much to promote its growth. Not only did Greg and he discuss the game intelligently for years, but Mr Nolan was never dictatorial. He always encouraged Greg to think of the why and the how as well as the when, which can be applied to the who and the where.

Greg is an astute analyst of the game. When he scored a century against the Queensland Colts a cricket identity came up to him and said, 'Well done.' Greg pointed out that the opposing captain had not placed his fieldsmen wisely and this had made the getting of the century a far easier task than it might otherwise have been. If for instance the captain had moved this fieldsman to that position and that fieldsman to this position Greg figured he might not have even scored a century. Greg would also lead from in front. His example and enthusiasm would be even more inspirational if the time came to be captain.

Gordon Nolan always told Greg he should try and be number one at everything he did. But its not politic to push one's own barrow for leadership. When George Negus asked him about the captaincy on '60 Minutes', Greg treated the question with care and said after seeing the affect it had had on Kim Hughes he did not know. When the subject came up on the car on the way to the physio's Greg said, 'I hardly ever think about it. Except when someone asks me.'

Back to the 1986 cricket season and the tour to New Zealand. Greg started the tour well when he scored his third Test century of the season in the First Test. His 130 was his highest score in a Test match.

But after that he just could not get it all together. In the Christchurch Test he made six and three. In the final Test he made five and four and Australia lost the series two to one.

Losing the last Test in New Zealand was the worst defeat of Greg's life. Australia as a young side really had the chance to win the series and establish some credibility. But when they lost the whole show seemed to lose momentum, which partially explains why Australia did so poorly in the first two one-dayers.

Greg can't quite understand his slump. Maybe the pressure of being in the spotlight got to him, maybe the crowds got to him, maybe his injured shoulder put him off. He can't put his finger on it, but the bottom line is he did not perform. You can have a thousand excuses but none of them mean a thing when you don't perform.

One man who may have enjoyed seeing Greg slip is Jeremy Coney, the New Zealand captain. Greg never succeeded in developing any social rapport with Coney whatsoever, but nonetheless Greg respects the man's ability as a cricketer. 'He didn't play well', Greg said, 'he played fantastic in New Zealand.'

Greg says he has hardly ever been involved in any but the most subtle sledging in the first class cricket. It just does not seem right in that field. It is not the way the great players of the eighties operate. Viv Richards and Ian Botham intimidate the opposition without even opening their mouths. Their demeanour shows their class. Richards is the man and his walk reflects it.

One of the rare incidents where Greg did become involved in a sledging match was with Coney in Western Australia. Coney told Greg he was no good and Greg saw red. They exchanged words. Dirk Wellham recalls Greg trying to stare down Coney. The incident does not register with Greg.

Coney was not the only New Zealander to have problems with Greg's approach. The New Zealand public hated him. 'Matthews has been subjected to a tirade of abuse wherever he has visited these past five weeks' Mike Coward wrote. 'On and off the ground, he has been mocked, taunted, teased, denounced and insulted. Apparently he is being penalised, persecuted, discriminated against – call it what you will – for being unconventional in a conventional and conservative society. While his behaviour on and off the field has been exemplary, he has been swamped by a wave of aggression and loathing.'

It happened everywhere. When Greg and the team went to a pub in Wellington to promote an Australian beer he had a full can thrown at him. At the grounds banners were put up abusing Greg. Police pulled down some of the more obnoxious including: 'What do Greg Matthews and Rock Hudson have in common?';Greg Matthews Aussie Closet Epileptic; Matthews for the Next Shuttle Mission. It was Matthews who Ate the Baby.' Neita Matthews says the banners were incited by a competition which rewarded the most outrageous anti-Matthews banner.

'Here', Greg said in New Zealand, 'I've received an enormous amount of hassles when I am out socially . . . why it has happened I don't know, they are a different society, a different people. I don't really want to comment too much. It's not my place to, it is their country and I am a visitor here. I'm a guest, and if they see fit to treat me that way, who am I to hassle them about it.'

Greg signed an incredible number of autographs in New Zealand. During breaks in play Greg would place a chair outside the dressing room and sign autographs for hours. He saw it as part of his cricketing responsibility.

People would ask, 'Where's Greg?'

The reply would invariably come, 'Outside signing autographs.'

'It was as though he was trying to win over the New Zealanders', Dave Gilbert said.

One young kid asked Greg for an autograph. Greg looked up and recognised him as someone who had thrown an egg at him. It was one of the few autographs Greg refused to sign. Despite his attention to those who worship him, Greg claims he has never had any heroes and has never asked for autographs.

But New Zealand was not all disaster in the public relations department. Four players, including Greg, stayed back for a charity match at the end of the tour. There were 15,000 people in the stands and when Greg walked out to bat they gave him a standing ovation.

More importantly Greg had won over his teammates. 'I get on well with them socially now because they know me better. We have a few beers and talk about life with Sanyo . . . and cricket and sex, drugs and rock and roll and everything. Before, the team was very established. They were used to leading a certain lifestyle for a number of years and I was the new person in the mini-society that is cricket.'

When I asked Greg in the car what he thought of his rapport with

the team, he said, 'No-one tells me to shut up, so I must be doing something right.'

We pull up outside Greg's new Paddington house.

'What do you think?'

I say great, even though it looks like any other Paddington terrace.

We then find the house that Errol's father bought. Greg asks me what I think of it. It looks ok to me, fairly big and light, so I say it looks pretty good. Greg says it is a bit over the top.

'You really are a funny bugger', I say to Greg. 'Whatdaya mean. Funny peculiar or funny ha ha.'

'A bit of both. You are a different person. An enigma, I can't put my finger on it. You are a real character.'

The conversation lags. Greg obviously does not want to pursue this. It is time for the next cricket question. I ask him about the up and coming series against England. He is all anticipation.

'If I only score one more Test century in my life, I want it to be against England. Of course I really want to score a 100 against the West Indies, but I really want to do it against England. The West Indies are the best but England are the one. That's what crickets all about ... the Ashes ... All the traditions ... They are the ones Australians love to beat.'

Greg is into anticipation. And also reflection.

He mentions that he enjoys holidays more in anticipation and reflection than while he is on them.

I say it is better to live in the present.

We pull up at his apartment. 'Have you got enough information?' Greg asks.

I think so.

'Well you should. You said you wanted an hour and you got three.'

Greg disappears into his apartment.

I sit and reflect on Greg Matthews. He's right. Reflection is enjoyable. And when you think of Greg Matthews, Australian cricketer, so is anticipation.

EPILOGUE: THE STUFF OF LEGENDS

The New York Giants baseball team were running fifth in their league. They were a team of also rans, who seemed to be out of their league. The Giants were playing the Brooklyn Dodgers.

The manager did not let Willie Mayes, the centre fielder, in to play until the fifth innings of the nine-innings game. Mayes' first time at bat saw him hit a home run. Then he jogged to centre field and caught a hit which on any other day would have got the batter to third base. A few innings later Mayes came racing in sliding on his chest to catch a ball just before it hit the first blade of grass. A run was saved. Other players nodded, gaped and grinned. Willie was back. All of a sudden a no-hoper team were unstoppable.

The American sportswriter, Roger Kahn, wrote, 'I have not again seen such an instant transformation in baseball, and as the season progressed it was not only Willie's tremendous play that kept the Giants driving and winning. His limitless enthusiasm touched everyone. Show up early. Play pepper, giggling and betting Cokes. Turn centre field into a garden. Then return to Harlem and play stick ball with neighbourhood children until darkness.'

Willie would be always hustling for extra base, always trying to steal any advantage, always sprinting after the impossible catch and always smiling and enjoying himself like a big kid in a sandlot. He inspired people outside his team. Some admirers named their children after him. Others wrote songs about him.

The team's mood rose with the star. 'When Willie is out there,' Sal Maglie, a great right hand hitter, said, 'all I gotta do is keep the ball in the park.'

The Giants beat a stronger Dodgers team for the pennant in their division. They advanced to the World Series against the seemingly invincible Cleveland Indians. The Giants were about to lose the first game of the World Series when Vic Wertz hit a high line drive to centre. It seemed a certain scoring shot. No-one could possibly get to it. Never say no-one again. Mayes turned and ran hell for leather with his back to the ball. There was no time to look. He could not have seen it. He timed his run perfectly and somehow the ball dropped over his shoulders into his hand. The play should not have happened. The play is famous. The Giants won the World Series in four straight games.

'Hard trainers and highly motivated types really can have such an impact on a team', Michael Whitney said. 'If a couple of those sort of guys are out, the feeling changes. Guys who really put in on the field are invaluable. We miss Greg a lot when he is not there, his enthusiasm and the way he puts out on the field. I have never seen the guy fall asleep.'

Bill O'Reilly said, 'Matthews . . . embraces all the qualities that we admire so much in the heroes who have graced our cricket fields since this country began . . . He is the one person presently entrenched in our game who possesses the divine touch that will fill our cricket grounds again without the help of that pantomine pastime so many people think is adding meaning to our national pastime . . . I am completely converted. I admit without the slightest reservation that I am prepared to field beside him in the slips all day long without seeking the friendly help of an ear plug. I am on his side. I congratulate all those kids who beat me so smartly to the point.'

ACKNOWLEDGEMENTS

Greg and I were at his house when the phone rang. It was Dirk Wellham. 'What's happening,' Greg said. 'Uh huh . . . What do you make of this Roland Fishman . . . You have only talked to him over the phone . . . I was just interested to know what you thought of him . . . Really!' A spot of laughter and then Greg moves on to the next subject. He finishes the call with, 'Later.'

By the time I got around to asking Greg what Wellham had said, he said he had forgotten. When I recounted the incident to Wellham, he laughed and said it was typical Greg.

Since I began this book many people have come up to me and asked, 'What is Greg Matthews really like?'

It is hard to say.

'Come on you must know. You must have spent a fair amount of time with him.'

As Neita said, Greg is just different. He has his good and bad points. He can be infuriatingly egocentric and endearingly generous. Life with or around him is never dull. He makes things happen. He would be great company for a night on the town, but a bit hard to take on a desert island. As a sportsman he is an inspiration, a great fighter, a born leader and the sort of person I would always want on my team. But don't ask me to put him in a neat box.

The man credited with being the first to identify the importance of the John F. Kennedy mystique, Norman Mailer, said: 'People who are always looking for solutions to everybody's personalities are second-rate citizens. It's very easy to understand second-rate people, they function on simple governing principles. They like to dominate experience with language, like to put everything in its place, label everything. Whereas first-rate people are impossible to understand. And very often it is impossible to understand second-rate people with first-rate qualities.'

So, it is much easier just to thank people. I am grateful for the great physical and emotional support of John Curtain, Sarah Sargent and my mother, Joan Fishman.

What made this book a pleasure to research was the frankness of the people I spoke to, particularly Jillian, Neita, brother Peter, Dirk Wellham, Oaksie, Dave Gilbert, Bill O'Reilly, Bob Simpson, Michael Snell, Michael Whitney and above all Greg, who, of course, made the process fun and dramatic.

Photo Credits
The publishers wish to thank the Matthews family and Jillian Clarke for providing photographs from their personal collections and John Fairfax and Sons Ltd for permission to reproduce the work of their photographers on the following pages: Mervyn Bishop 20; Geoff Bull 22; Gerrit Fokkema 1, 54; Craig Golding 34; Stephen Holland 168; Tom Linsen 17; Phil Lock 125; Stephen Lunam 68; Nigel McNeil 173; Paul Mathews 87, 90, 139, 141, 155, 178; Peter Morris 84, 100, 130, 146, 151, 160, 165; Robert Pearce 42, 65; Alan Purcell 15; Barry Stevens 157; Rick Stevens 24, 31, 117, 148; Ross Willis 121. Particular thanks are due to Virginia Eddy of the John Fairfax Feature Bureau for her enthusiastic and cheerful professionalism.